Healthcare at a Turning Point

A Roadmap for Change

Endorsements

Everyone agrees that the American healthcare system needs to change, but there is little agreement about how it should change. Abrams and Numerof paint a picture of how healthcare could look in an ideal future, and show manufacturers, payers, and providers a way to get there. Examining the healthcare system today, changes already taking place in attitudes toward innovation and medical education...they demonstrate how the key players in healthcare must change their thinking to survive. ...The main, and certainly provocative, message: If we move to a value-based system built on patient choice, rather than a cost-based system that assumes one size fits all, the consumer of healthcare is the ultimate beneficiary.

The book will stimulate the thinking of industry across functions, and should be read not only by management but by R&D, strategic planning, and sales. Sections on the need to form partnerships and alliances can change the way industry, payers, and providers think about each other. By examining the four forces they see as dominating our healthcare environment today, namely, changes in the regulatory environment, a changing competitive landscape, shifting technology, and changing market expectations, Abrams and Numerof have indeed provided an insightful guide to how industry needs to change its strategic thinking.

David L. Horwitz, MD, PhD, FACP
Chief Medical Officer
Johnson & Johnson Diabetes Institute

Here it is in *Healthcare at a Turning Point*: U.S. healthcare must restore control and accountability for intimate personal decisions to each of us as our own consumer. No one else can define our quality–value–price equation, and discipline our providers... Such is the economics, humanity, history and even politic of western innovation...it is time for a Renaissance of those principles, just as articulated here in *Healthcare at a Turning Point*.

Steve Bonner
President and Chief Executive Officer
Cancer Treatment Centers of America®

Numerof and Abrams have conducted a thorough analysis of the implications of market and non-market forces on all players in the health industry—carriers, care providers, governments, consumers and employers. They have hit the nail on the head that it will take disruptive innovation and a collaborative approach across all these stakeholders to drive solutions to the fundamental problems of high cost and poor quality in healthcare.

I appreciate that Numerof and Abrams focus in on three major principles: 1. Rethink the customer: It's really the consumer, the end-user of healthcare services. The consumer needs to be at the center of the work that we are undertaking. It is imperative that we provide them transparency of cost, quality, and value. 2. Watch out for nontraditional competitors: There are many other industries that have been historically very close to the consumer. The players in our industry are changing, and all of those who serve the consumer need to rapidly evolve ourselves in order to differentiate and succeed. 3. Segment care providers: We need to apply the discipline of market segmentation to our relationships with care providers. That is, we cannot assume that a one-size-fits-all approach on paying for value or outcome will succeed with each and every physician or hospital. Rather, we must segment our networks and identify which care providers are most likely to succeed in a partnership to reform payment in a particular way, work with them closely and then allow that success to breed other success in the marketplace.

Elena McFann
VP Network Strategy and Implementation
UnitedHealthcare

The authors present thought-provoking ideas for the "disruptive innovation" needed to uncover pragmatic solutions for our country's healthcare delivery system. Though I don't agree with all they have written, this suggested blueprint for market-based action is a must-read for all sides of the healthcare reform debate.

Marc Boutin
Executive Vice President & Chief Operating Officer
National Health Council

Numerof and Abrams have crafted a thoughtful, and often provocative, analysis of the challenges and opportunities facing the healthcare industry today. At its heart is a clarion call for the sector to become much more patient- and consumer-centric—before their existing business models become obsolete.

Paul Howard
Director and Senior Fellow
Center for Medical Progress
Manhattan Institute for Policy Research

For every professional engaged in the financing and delivery of medical care, this book is essential. Like it or not, sparked by the renewed debate over the controversial Affordable Care Act, we find ourselves in the midst of a major transformation in the healthcare sector of the economy. The convergence of biomedical breakthroughs, new medical technologies, and new organizational structures is upon us. But the authors got it right: change will be frustrating, and energies will be diverted into unproductive channels, unless and until we change healthcare financing and put the patient in the center of the process as the key decision-maker.

Robert E. Moffit, PhD
Senior Fellow, Center for Policy Innovation
The Heritage Foundation

Have there ever been two not-so-little words that turned an industry upside down, virtually paralyzed the planning process and left providers and consumers alike adrift as much as "healthcare reform"? The authors bring a calm, dispassionate tone to the dialogue, underscoring the unsettling nature of transition (a far more palatable word than change) and offer reasonable strategies that override politics. I found the emphasis on collaboration especially comforting and doable.

Ellen Sherberg
Publisher
St. Louis Business Journal

...(I)t is important to have a clear bridge between the issues of today and the possibility of a much brighter future. Without glossing over serious issues...this book describes a way forward for those inside and outside the healthcare system.

Jeff Thompson, MD
Chief Executive Officer
Gundersen Lutheran Health System

Healthcare at a Turning Point

A Roadmap for Change

Rita E. Numerof, PhD
Michael N. Abrams, MA

Foreword by David B. Nash, MD, MBA

CRC Press
Taylor & Francis Group
Boca Raton   London   New York

CRC Press is an imprint of the
Taylor & Francis Group, an **informa** business

A PRODUCTIVITY PRESS BOOK

This book is dedicated to Dr. Paul Numerof,
whose pioneering work in medical innovation
and willingness to challenge the status quo have
been a source of inspiration and support.

Contents

Foreword

Because healthcare is really at a turning point, we have to ask the question, to whom should we turn for advice? Where should we go for help in facing the four seismic shifts that are affecting the healthcare industry? Those shifts include significant changes in the regulatory environment, a dynamic and rapidly changing competitive landscape, shifts in technology and changing market expectations. I hope many readers will turn to Rita Numerof and Michael Abrams in their new book. I'm glad I turned to Numerof and Abrams for advice!

Numerof and Abrams are astute observers of these aforementioned seismic shifts affecting our industry. They have a keen ear for hearing those hoof beats in the distance. They have overcome what I call "mural dyslexia"—the inability to read the handwriting on the wall!

Healthcare at a Turning Point takes some unpopular positions. It confronts some unpleasant truths. Let me outline a few of these "truths" as I see them. Hospitals are not in the wellness business and as a result, a transformation of hospitals as the source of wellness and prevention in the 21st century is probably wrong-headed.

Information technology, while critically important, is not the "fix" that it has been held up to be. In fact, most progress in information technology is all about the billing, with very few products to support significant improvements in the value of the care we deliver.

Although comparative effectiveness research (CER) finally has a home in a quasi-public new federal agency, it probably cannot overcome the lack of transparency within the hospital marketplace. It still cannot help discern differences in outcomes from one institution to another. And because hospital revenue will be less and less focused on procedures, it's hard for any observer to link CER to improvements in outcomes and improvements in competitiveness.

Accountable Care Organizations are simply not the answer. Giving patients the power to make better choices and incenting them economically to do so will drive the bulk of change in the system.

While hospitals upgrade various "product lines," it may turn out to be their downfall due to increasing regulatory pressure. Every major integrated delivery system is focused on neurosurgery, cancer care and cardiology; exactly the areas that will continue to be highly regulated, especially in the inpatient setting. Even the organizations that pay the bills for this inpatient care, outside of Medicare, are under crushing regulatory reform.

Finally, bundled payment will work because it is the only tool that adequately aligns incentives among providers and among patients and gives economic power to the marketplace; the greatest innovative engine in the world!

So now let me answer my rhetorical question as to where to turn. All of the aforementioned, critical take-home messages lie at the heart of *Healthcare at a Turning Point*. Many will ignore these signals on the road to progress. They will ignore these signals are their peril. Numerof and Abrams have given us a roadmap for success, but their voices will be drowned out by the louder voices wedded to the status quo.

Organizations courageous enough to embrace *Healthcare at a Turning Point* will be glad that they did. They will benefit from powerful insights that go against the current dogma.

Kudos to Numerof and Abrams for *Healthcare at a Turning Point*, at a real turning point in our industry! I know where I will turn for advice, and I hope many readers will as well.

David B. Nash, MD, MBA

Acknowledgments

In thinking about who to thank or acknowledge along the journey to writing this book, the list was a bit overwhelming. So many people we've touched in the last several years have had an impact by challenging our thinking, agreeing with and extending our ideas, or introducing us to like-minded people committed to bringing about a new business model that reflects more value and better outcomes in what is arguably one of the most important sectors in our society.

At the top of our list has to be our dedicated team at Numerof & Associates, Inc. (NAI). Each member of this incredibly hard-working, talented, and creative group has been subjected to or participated in spirited discussions leading to papers, many of which have found their way into the book. As an industry in transition, healthcare is at the core of our work. So the book is informed by our practice, by our clients, and by the firm's writing. It is also informed by confidential discussions with congressional leaders and their staffs whose openness to our challenges reinforced our ideas and propelled us to write this story.

When Kim White, a member of NAI's consulting team, agreed to go to dinner with Rita last summer to help her organize the material for the book, we were not sure she had any idea what she'd signed on for! She masterfully led our efforts to select a publisher, and guided the development of what became a winning proposal. Her extraordinary project management skills were taken to new heights and her influential style made weekend and late night writing, organizing, and proofing sessions fun. We can't thank her enough for her commitment and personal dedication to the project.

Vicki Mertz, a key member of our operations team, deserves our special thanks. She worked long hours making sure the manuscript was clean. Always the perfectionist, Vicki pointed out tense match discrepancies, needed citations, and other critical details. On the research side, we want to thank Dan King and Matt Levy for helping to ensure our citations were up to date, and for searching out key facts to illustrate points we wanted to drive home. Jill Sackman, Norm Numerof, Steve Rothenberg, and Bill Ott—authors, coauthors, and contributors on many of our published writings that have found their way into the book—have been active participants in the strategy discussions that have helped shape our views. Our spirited debates have informed our thinking and enriched our ideas.

Beyond the NAI team, special thanks go to Ellen Sherberg, publisher of the *St. Louis Business Journal*, who made sure that some of the controversial ideas that we represent got a voice. We are indebted to Paul Howard with the Manhattan Institute and Bob Moffit with the Heritage Foundation for their encouragement, support, and willingness to engage in spirited debate about the subject of healthcare. On the policy and legislative side, Rita would like to thank some very special people who believed early on in the value of our thinking—Congressman Todd Akin, Senator Roy Blunt, former Senate Majority Leader Tom Daschle, former Speaker of the House Newt Gingrich, and many other legislators on both sides of the aisle in the House and Senate. We'd be remiss in not thanking some very special people who initially saw the value of our ideas—Julie Eckstein, Lauren Ellis, and Debbie Cochran—as well as many other legislative staffers whom Rita has been privileged to work with over the years.

Introduction

Embarking on the Journey

The journey to this book began in the summer of 2008 in the run-up to the presidential election. As committed voters, we watched the debates and listened intently to the political speeches of the Democratic and Republican hopefuls. Our ears perked up when the subject turned to healthcare, and it frequently did. Given that it was a subject we both knew quite a bit about—we'd been consulting across the industry globally for almost two decades—it was disturbing when we heard solutions being proposed that we knew didn't have a snowball's chance of fixing the serious, underlying problems that *had* to be addressed. We knew that healthcare delivery was fragmented, confusing, opaque, expensive, and sometimes downright dangerous—anything but consumer centric. While it made sense that information technology (IT) would be seen as playing *a* role in any ultimate solution, it was outrageous to suggest—as most of the hopefuls did—that IT was *the* solution. It was, however, an appealing cry that wouldn't likely offend anyone; in that regard it was politically "safe" and unlikely to alienate potential voters—safe but misleading.

From our perspective the real underlying issues weren't being addressed, in large part because the right questions weren't being asked. Since IT was being offered as the solution to an expensive, broken healthcare system in this country, then one basic question would have to be, why didn't the industry introduce IT to help modernize itself and create more efficiencies just like other industries did? The short answer is that it didn't matter, in large part because the root problem wasn't IT, it was a more fundamental one—it was about payment: who pays, how, and what gets paid for. Ironically, healthcare delivery organizations used technology well when it came to ensuring they got paid. It mattered there. But to coordinate care, to drive improvement in outcomes and lower cost, technology wasn't used. Even in those organizations that had invested millions in data warehouses, there was far too often a profound reluctance to meaningfully change behavior. Or the data was available, but people lacked the ability to package it in a way that made it easily accessible to improve outcomes. As we argue here, the reasons for this are multifaceted, but until they're understood, it's unlikely that the fundamental changes we need will take place.

In the fall of 2008 we had just completed a project for a major pharmaceutical manufacturer. It was a time of intense scrutiny of that segment of the industry by Congress, the Department of Justice, and a number of other interested parties, including academic medical centers. The business environment was particularly hostile to pharma; continuing medical education (CME) was in the crosshairs. Subpoenas were issued regularly, and the underlying issue centered on conflict of interest. In a nutshell, the industry was criticized for unfairly influencing physicians to prescribe drugs of "questionable" value. The influence came in the form of payment— often for participation in clinical trials, speakers' bureaus, paid continuing medical education, and the proverbial branded trinkets. Lots of legislation ensued, and manufacturers are now required to report payments to doctors of greater than $10 or more than $100 in aggregate per year. What was often missed in the intense rhetoric were the thinly veiled agendas of players across the board.

Academic researchers and the medical centers that paid them positioned themselves as pure and objective, because they are nonprofits, and many wanted to keep manufacturers from calling on doctors at all. And they had a lot to gain in this scenario. Essentially, they were positioning themselves as the gatekeepers for medical information and CME.

It was at this time that Rita had a chance to speak off-line with a pharmaceutical executive who had recently held a senior administrative post in one of the key federal agencies concerned with healthcare. She laid out a picture of the environment she saw unfolding—that the government was headed down a path intended to slow innovation, and moving to get more and more Americans on a government-based single-payer system with the ultimate objective of reducing access. We were, after all, facing the crush of baby boomers and a limited amount of money. Expecting (and secretly hoping) to be told she was just being paranoid, Rita was shocked when the executive's reaction was quite the opposite—that the picture she'd painted was an accurate one and few realized it. Armed with that disturbing piece of insight, we became convinced that we had an obligation to attempt to influence the debate. We didn't like where the train was headed; we knew we needed healthcare reform in this country, and we became committed to trying to make a difference.

By the spring of 2009, Rita became an advisor to a number of congressional leaders, bringing a strategic and systemic set of solutions—rational insights into what needs to change if we're going to crack the code and fix the underlying problems across this critical industry. We are "equal opportunity critics" and recognize that the business model of the industry needs to change and *is* now changing. We have spoken and written extensively on the subject, advocating for a consumer-driven market model, a position we first articulated more than twenty years ago. The time is right—2,700 pages of legislation and thousands more pages of rules aren't the solution, but at least the legislation has forced an important dialogue. Despite the partisan rhetoric surrounding the Supreme Court verdict upholding the constitutionality of the Affordable Care Act and the controversial individual mandate, we *need* healthcare reform in this country. What it will mean for every segment of this essential industry is the subject of this book.

The journey has been personally exciting, challenging, rewarding, and humbling for each of us. We hope our insights provide perspective. We are all in this together, and together we believe we can bring about the changes needed to improve our nation's health.

Rita Numerof, PhD
and
Michael N. Abrams, MA
Saint Louis, Missouri

Chapter 1

A Vision for Tomorrow

Vision of a Fundamentally Different Future

It's the year 2023. It's hard to believe that just a decade ago there was intense debate about healthcare in the United States. Today, we have more options than were ever available before. We spend less on healthcare delivery, and we seem to be generally healthier as a nation. Costs have come down dramatically in some sectors of the industry, and dynamic new businesses have sprung up to meet emerging needs. Traditional businesses have evolved with core components repurposed. Financing mechanisms have changed, and while not perfect, there is better alignment between cost and quality. There is better coordination of care, more personal accountability for health outcomes, more choice and competition, fewer restrictions, and generally less intervention and fewer procedures.

Of course, there have been some business "casualties" across the industry, as those organizations that held on to old models found themselves unable to adapt and therefore unable to compete in a new marketplace.

Medical tourism is up as the United States has once more become the global destination for elective procedures and continues to be the gold standard for complex care. Innovations here have been taken to other parts of the globe as researchers in the United States continue to work collaboratively with their global counterparts to find ways to improve health outcomes. New investments in research and development (R&D) have had big payoffs, as medical interventions have replaced surgery, and in some cases minimally invasive surgical procedures have replaced chronic medical treatment. Equally important, non-Western approaches to treatment have gained acceptance as the evidence for their efficacy is increasingly demonstrated.

Everyone in the United States has access to health insurance. Typically, it's attached to the person, although there are still some sectors of the economy where employer-based healthcare is the preferred option. National access opened up competition. Local providers sprang up, sometimes coordinated with more traditional care delivery organizations, which together built comprehensive or "bundled" approaches to disease management, wellness, and prevention. Whereas fragmentation and inefficiency still characterized healthcare in 2012, coordination and cost effectiveness increasingly characterize the industry. Of course, there are still niche players who are quite successful in their market segments.

What's so remarkable is the creativity brought to bear on what appeared in 2012 to be intractable problems that some argued could only be fixed by a single, government payer. Indeed, the creation of true market-based solutions, with very targeted policy (government) intervention, has enabled this magnitude of change in such a relatively short period of time.

Insurance payment reform enabled interstate access and reduced complicated rules and bureaucratic inefficiency. Member retention, once a major problem for the industry, due in part to an overreliance on employer-based benefit coverage, has dramatically increased in recent years. Whereas average member retention was once pegged at 18–24 months, it continues to increase, with some carriers reporting averages of 6–8 years and a positive trend line. Portability is characteristic of all insurance since most individuals hold their own policies, with myriad design options for consumers to choose from—long-term care, full coverage including vitamins and over-the-counter (OTC) products, basic catastrophic coverage, and specialty options including 10- , 20- , and 30-year life support.

Pooling and tax incentives have leveled the playing field and made this a reality. True competition has lowered costs and increasingly put consumers in the driver's seat. Employers, where they do provide coverage, have almost entirely moved to defined contribution approaches. Employers get to make the determination of what the contribution will be—not the insurance provider or the government. For insurers still in the business, the model has moved to a retail individual-dominated market.

On the delivery side, things are very different. Fundamental to change has been a shift in a basic assumption of the industry—that volume (or at least a certain type of volume based on payer and procedure) is good. In the world of the healthcare continuum—prevention, early diagnosis, intervention, and rehab—traditional hospitalization volume represents a cost, not revenue! Not wanting to repeat the mistakes of capitation in the 1980s, 2012 innovators committed to short- and long-term health outcomes.

This required enormous behavioral change on the part of physicians, social agencies, and consumers. It also required new approaches to metrics and the generation of evidence. Increasingly, healthcare delivery institutions are focused on optimal outcomes—the right treatment(s) in the right amount, administered in the right way, at the right time, at the right place, for the right patient. Hospitals are less frenetic for caregivers, and they tend to focus more on the things they do best—acute, complex intervention, often in specialty institutions. They are less likely to attempt to be "all things to all people."

Nurses who frequently focused in 2012, on getting through the shift without hurting anyone, now focus on the bedside—on consumer and family education, on rehab, on care management, coordination, and health outcomes—and a smooth transition back into the home and community.

Hospital-acquired infection rates, while never reaching zero, have been dramatically reduced; medication errors also are down below 1%. No longer are hospitals generally recognized as unsafe.

Together with the elimination of redundant and unnecessary care, estimated at between 30% and 40% at some of the best hospitals even in 2012, these changes resulted in the savings that enabled innovation and universal coverage without adding cost.

The refusal of the Centers for Medicare and Medicaid Services (CMS) to pay for such error-based *never events* initially forced healthcare delivery institutions to dramatically change practice—or suffer the financial consequences. Similarly, 30-day readmission payment restrictions drove better coordination within the hospital setting and facilitated discharge planning and coordination with community agencies and post-acute care settings. Discharge planning now starts pre-admission except in the case of emergent situations, and even there, it begins at the time of admission. Commercial insurers, not surprisingly, followed CMS's lead.

On the physician front, frightening trends in primary care have been reversed. With balanced payment increasingly recognizing the enormous contribution and broad system expertise of primary care physicians and a decrease in compensation for narrow *specialty* care, more physicians have been going into primary care medicine as a specialty, thus reversing the disturbing trend in 2012. Where there were significant shortages projected years out for primary care physicians in 2012, now more than 20% have selected this specialty area in 2023. Contrary to what was anticipated, the small business model for independent physicians continues, nurse practitioners have opened offices, and integrated cross-specialty practice models have emerged to offer their customers comprehensive healthcare solutions accessible to local communities. Increasingly, consumers get care they need in their homes, at retail clinics, and sometimes at the office...when they need it.

In 2012 defensive medicine was frequently offered as a major contributor to the problem of overutilization. Essentially, physicians and hospitals felt as though they needed to leave no stone unturned in diagnosis and treatment to protect against potential legal liability. Some patients, unencumbered by the need to actually pay for the services, would likewise demand that no stone be left unturned, even when the downside risk outweighed the upside potential. Clinical judgment was painted as a prisoner of the legal system, and tort reform became the obstacle to rational resource utilization. How things have changed in just a few short years.

Today, increased transparency, reliance on evidence, change in payment mechanisms and the redefinition of the consumer's role in health care decisions have dramatically changed the picture. Patients are more likely to collaborate with their physicians, especially primary care providers, and evidence is used to determine which tests need to be done and when.

In the midst of this change, some hospitals have repurposed bricks and mortar, turning low-occupancy beds into assisted living long-term care (LTC) and long-term acute care hospitals (LTACHs). Still others have created temporary residences for families visiting sick relatives receiving needed treatment and rehabilitation.

New players, not in the traditional healthcare space, created dramatic disruption by taking advantage of the industry's inability to see itself in a fundamentally different business model. Primary care began moving, ever so slowly, to walk-in clinics in retail settings in 2010 and 2011, picking up speed dramatically in 2012 and 2013. More and more people turned to convenience and began to trust nontraditional settings for blood pressure and other screenings, flu shots and other immunizations, and even nonurgent care.

Screenings have led to earlier diagnoses and referrals to specialists. Industry leaders including Walmart, Walgreens, and CVS shook up the industry. Capitalizing on location, they brought the health clinic into the retail space, tying in low-cost access to generic prescription medications and store brand over-the-counter products. Their enormous success also disrupted traditional pharmacy benefit managers (PBMs) who, in retrospect, have been a bridge between the old and new model of healthcare.

It's truly a different world!

Seeds of Disruption

Getting to a new future isn't easy. But if it can't be envisioned, then it can't be realized. Typically, the move to anything radically different is sparked by a catalyst. But for the catalyst to work, the environment for change has to be prepared. The Patient Protection and Affordable Care Act (PPACA) served as the catalyst.

The PPACA legislation of 2010 reflects the largest appropriation of power from the individual to the administrative branch in our country's history. It has provoked phenomenal controversy in an industry that has been loath to change. It has accelerated industry *transition*—that painful process that forces market leaders to rethink their business models and allows new entrants, unencumbered by "the way we've always done it before," to become the market leaders of the future. The seeds of disruptive innovation are around us, beckoning to the truly innovative and threatening those wedded to the past. Fortunately, healthcare isn't the only industry to undergo fundamental transformation, and there are important insights to be learned from the experience of others.

Healthcare Isn't the First Industry in Transition

Some of the best insights can be learned from the experience of IBM, now a global leader, with more than $100 billion in sales and approximately 425,000 employees. But in the late 1980s, IBM was close to bankruptcy.

In the early 1980s, IBM was dominant; it focused on mainframe computing, the "big iron" purchased by large corporations. The company enjoyed approximately 50% gross margins on mainframes and the lion's share of worldwide industry profits. It had a bullish future. Long-term projections were pegged at over $200 billion in sales. The company also enjoyed a stellar reputation and strong brand position—"Nobody ever got fired for buying IBM." In 1985 the company was, in the words of its new CEO, John Akers, "successful beyond [its] wildest expectations."

However, in just a few years, IBM flirted with bankruptcy, and between 1991 and 1993 reported over $24 billion in restructuring charges. IBM ignored the warning signs that the market was moving away from mainframes, holding on to the belief that the business computer was, and always would be, the mainframe. Their assumption was that PCs were for small businesses and home computing—at the desk and in the kitchen. As IBM saw it, mainframes had great margins and proprietary technology and IBM had solid customer relationships and market-leading products. PCs, on the other hand, were a niche invention, with "upstart" companies coming onto the scene.

As we all know, the PC wasn't just a niche product. It was the business model of the future. Even though IBM was widely credited with inventing the PC, the company didn't fully appreciate the shift in the market. IBM wound up nearly bankrupt and endured a painful and difficult restructuring.

When hardware sales tanked, IBM's survival strategy was services, which had been the sweetener in its mainframe heyday. Ironically, services became the bread and butter of their business model and the bridge to their PC-based business. The IBM case demonstrates the need to know what's happening in the market and *in adjacent spaces*, understand the implications, and take the right actions to protect market leadership. Most importantly, it demonstrates the risk inherent in organizational arrogance, too frequently the blind spot of market leaders who erroneously believe they can't be unseated because they're so dominant.

Perhaps less dramatic, but nonetheless painful for those involved, have been recent disruptions in the travel and real estate industries. Travelocity and Expedia, both created in 1996, offer a window into an industry disrupted by technology. Travelocity, a subsidiary of Sabre Holdings, a division of American Airlines, revolutionized consumers' ability to compare and purchase tickets directly, without going through travel agents or brokers. It was the first website that allowed consumer access to Sabre's schedule and fare information, becoming more popular once AOL's travel portal became associated with the Travelocity brand in 1999. At the same time, Expedia was launched by Microsoft, another online booking site that revolutionized how consumers researched and booked travel more generally. A small division in 1996, it was spun out in 1999, becoming a publically traded company on NASDAQ. It has grown dramatically since 2002, following InterActiveCorp's acquisition of a controlling interest in the company, and remains the world's leading online travel company, successfully disintermediating the traditional travel agent.

In real estate a similar dynamic has unfolded. The introduction of *for sale by owner* has taken a bite out of the profits of traditional real estate brokers. The model is attractive in that commissions are in the 1–2% range, not the traditional 6+% range that real estate brokers historically commanded.

In the publishing, music, and photography industries the dynamic is similar. Amazon disrupted the retail book sales world, while Apple Computer continues to disrupt through the creation of smart gadgets, replacing phones, cameras, calendars, and so on with smart phones.

In healthcare delivery disruption isn't entirely new, but the impact hasn't really been as well understood as it needs to be. Traditional hospital money makers have been dislodged and moved to other settings. Over the last fifteen years, entrepreneurial physicians and administrators, enabled by the emergence of new technology, have created free-standing specialty ambulatory care centers characterized by efficiency, convenience, and a consumer-centered model. Hospitals, struggling with silos and bureaucracy, have long recognized that they couldn't compete successfully with these more nimble enterprises, and in some cases exited these specialty niches altogether.

Conflict-of-interest charges brought against some of these entrepreneurs have significantly restricted what these groups can and can't do. Nowhere has the question of hospitals' vested interests in this really been in the public spotlight, maybe because they've been seen as too big to fail or perhaps another "third rail." In many areas around the country, hospitals have become the dominant employers; other business leaders sit on their boards and their employees are an important part of the electorate. As the move to a consumer model in healthcare takes shape, coupled with increasing concerns about cost, all players in the industry should take note of what this means.

Where Are We Currently?

Popular discontent with the healthcare system has grown so significantly that legislators and regulators have responded with new laws, new mandates, and additional coercive controls, unfortunately not recognizing that sometimes *less is more*. The 2010 healthcare reform legislation included broad experimentation, new payment methods, and new market mechanisms that could profoundly alter market dynamics for healthcare delivery, and all other segments of the industry, but not necessarily in a positive way.

Federal and state regulations are moving toward greater disclosure of clinical metrics, based on the premise that consumers should be able to evaluate quality as part of their decision-making process. New organizational structures have been promoted, for example, accountable care organizations (ACOs), almost as a desperate attempt to fix the looming challenges we face. The inherent problems with this are discussed in Chapter 5. New payment methods are also evolving that attempt to link payment to more specific and robust quality measures, cost efficiency, and patient outcomes. As an example, the 2012 Center for Medicare and Medicaid Innovation (CMMI) bundled pricing demonstration projects lay out a series of guidelines and different models that attempt to align physician and hospital charges, improve outcomes, and foster integration across the continuum of care.

Providers are under increasing pressure to improve quality and deliver care in new ways. At the heart of the problem is fee-for-service (FFS) payment, now broadly recognized as creating perverse incentives for hospitals and physicians to offer more treatments and more options than may be medically necessary. FFS doesn't currently reward efforts that would improve quality or prevent unnecessary utilization, like chronic disease management for diabetics to reduce Emergency room visits for low blood sugar reactions. A shift from FFS to a more accountable care model would mean a shift of responsibility for outcomes, increased sharing of risk for healthcare costs, and increased gain sharing as improvements are realized.

New delivery approaches are being piloted, like patient-centered medical homes (PCMHs) and ACOs, but the current excitement obscures the fact that many organizations lack the resources and capabilities to successfully implement them. Furthermore, CMS rules covering ACO governance models are enormously complicated and resource intensive, and rest on a faulty set of assumptions. Since treatments must be paid for, insurers and their network of providers have to work in tandem to implement new care delivery and payment models. And at the end of the day, consumers need to behave differently. In the chapters that follow, we explore how the industry got here, what the implications are for each of the major industry segments, and offer a plan for moving forward.

Chapter 2

Whose Agenda Controls Your Healthcare?

Why a Market-Based Model for Healthcare Is a Good Thing

In the fury of the healthcare debate, most people have come to realize that we spend a lot of money on healthcare in this country. It's also generally recognized that we aren't getting our money's worth. "Better health outcomes at lower cost" has become the common theme for efforts to reform healthcare.

So, why is this? It's partly because neither the physician nor the patient—the critical actors or decision makers in the equation—are paying for it. As a result, neither has a direct stake in the cost side of the equation.

Unlike other markets, third parties negotiate for and pay the costs of healthcare—businesses through the mechanism of benefits, and insurers through paying the bills. While it's generally understood that rising costs for healthcare benefits have had a dampening effect on wages, the concept is theoretical to most, generally because we have limited visibility to how this really works in practice. Nor do we understand how this dynamic impacts our purchasing power in the form of higher prices for goods and services in other markets—essentially a double whammy.

In every other industry, advancing technology has generally resulted in lower costs and improved products and services. It hasn't worked that way in healthcare.

Until we create a true market-based approach to the health-care industry, we won't be able to crack rising costs in any meaningful way. Transparency, increased accountability, and a consumer-centered model for healthcare will be table stakes to achieve the goal of better health outcomes at lower cost.

How Did We Get into This Mess?

Books will be written about all of the contributing factors to our current healthcare crisis. At the heart of the problem, how-ever, is the reality that *how we pay for healthcare drives what we get.*[1] This is how any free market works—or doesn't.

So, how did we get to this point? During World War II employers began offering benefits such as health insurance to attract and keep employees. Then, in 1954, Congress passed a law making employer contributions to these health plans tax deductible, without making the health benefits taxable to employees. This innocuous tax benefit not only encouraged the spread of catastrophic insurance, but also unintentionally encouraged the use of healthcare insurance for all expenses. The snowball continued to gain momentum when Medicare and Medicaid adopted the comprehensive insurance model as the basis for their payments. As a result, today many believe we need comprehensive health insurance for *all* care, and that even routine care is too expensive for us to handle on our own.

One of the most critical reform success factors, then, will be the proper alignment of payment with results—providing incentives for the right provider *and* consumer behaviors in order to achieve measurably better health outcomes. We need a new business model in the industry.

Any realistic effort to create an improved business model must comprehensively address the extraordinarily complex array of multiple stakeholders involved. In particular, this includes drug, device, and diagnostics manufacturers; hospital and physician providers; ourselves as consumers and payers (including the government). *Every one of these stakeholders is "at fault" for our current situation, including the consumer.*

- Manufacturers have focused on clinical value or equivalence as required for regulatory approval, and otherwise largely ignored economic value in their innovation of new drugs, medical devices, and tests. In every other industry, new technology has resulted in *more benefit at lower cost*. In healthcare, this has not been the case, as payments have not been tied to evidence of economic and clinical value.
- Providers have assumed a production mentality that has resulted in overutilization, uncoordinated care, and deteriorating quality. In the absence of payment tied to quality and cost management, the healthcare delivery industry is notably unique in its inability (or unwillingness) to change how it provides care in order to improve. Despite the industry oversight and accreditation of JCAHO (Joint Commission on Accreditation of Healthcare Organizations), most hospitals have not meaningfully improved quality or their value proposition. Nor have they taken a lead in coordinating care in their communities.
- Consumers are demanding drugs and procedures whether their physician says they need them or not. Over time, employer-based healthcare insurance has eroded any expectation or capability of consumers to make cost–benefit decisions on their own behalf, displacing this with a sense of entitlement for any service

they desire. Direct-to-consumer advertising by drug and device manufacturers has taken great advantage of this lack of accountability, encouraging patients in droves to "talk to their doctor" about any real or imagined ailment for which there is a product.

■ And in their interest to control costs, payers (especially the government) have devised a payment system that lacks any alignment with either better care or reduced costs. Worse, they have created a new administrative cost burden with a cost-accounting approach to payment that has spawned a new industry just to deal with the minutiae of billing—totally disconnected from any outcomes healthcare is supposed to achieve.

■ Finally, both the Centers for Medicare and Medicaid Services (CMS) and private payers, by virtue of their choice of payment rationale and business practices relative to providers, have contributed to a deterioration in the ethical standards of the entire healthcare sector.

CMS has chosen to underpay providers by 15–20% relative to market rates and the actual cost of care delivery as its way of managing costs. Because of its massive market power, providers have no choice but to accept this compensation, which naturally leaves them feeling abused. CMS also has established the business practice of paying the claims received promptly and relatively uncritically. Combined with a Byzantine pricing scheme, serves as an invitation to game the system through upcoding, which has become normative, and outright fraud, in other words widespread.

Private payers have taken the opposite tack. They scrutinize claims, challenging, denying, and downcoding payments. When combined with excessive payment delays, this again leaves providers feeling victimized, setting the stage for rationalization of any tactic they take that allows them to redress the financial humiliation forced on them.

The combination of these dynamics has created a situation in which physicians, hospitals, and even manufacturers more easily find excuses for overutilization of diagnostics and procedures; for devoting resources to building volume for those services that pay, rather than those that are needed; for gaming the system against the spirit, if not the letter of the law; and for using their own market clout to exact unreasonable concessions from their suppliers. The pervasive reach of payers and the impact of their respective practices have contributed to the ethical erosion of a profession historically energized by the most noble and ethical motives—a loss in other words is far more profound than any economic measure can capture.

As a result, the United States is paying more than any other country for healthcare (see Table 2.1), while national epidemics

Table 2.1 Total Health Expenditure by Country (per Capita)

Country	Population[a]	2009[b] ($)	2010[b] ($)
United States	309.0	7,960	8,327
Norway	50.5	5,352	5,887[c]
Switzerland	7.8	5,144	5,658[c]
Canada	34.1	4,363	4,799[c]
United Kingdom	61.3	3,487	3,836[c]
Spain	46.0	3,067	3,374
South Korea	50.5	1,879	1,980
Mexico	108.4	918	934

Source: Compiled from OECD Health Data 2011, Organization for Economic Cooperation and Development, Stats, oecd.org/index.aspx?DataSetCode=HEALTH_STAT.

[a] Population estimates in millions based on 2010 data.
[b] Numbers are per capita healthcare expenditures based on U.S. dollars.
[c] No 2010 data existed for these countries, so the numbers were based on a 10% average historic growth rate as reported for previous years.

such as diabetes and obesity rage out of control. All stakeholders are contributing to this situation, and all will need to be part of the solution.

A critical requirement for a free market to actually work is accountability for the cost consequences of decisions, in this case the treatment decisions between a physician and a consumer. Across stakeholders, this accountability is actually very difficult to find, and more the exception than the rule. As we have described, providers and consumers are driving unnecessary utilization that represents unnecessary costs. Quality is slipping, but providers expect to be compensated for fixing problems they've created. And private insurers have followed CMS's lead in lockstep to create a payment system that encourages overutilization rather than quality and cost control.

When we remove accountability for the consequences of our actions, we invite unintended negative consequences. The implementation of diagnosis-related groups (DRGs) by CMS in essence removed any organizational or individual responsibility for cost *and* quality decisions. The doctors who make the decisions generally don't have any stake in the cost to treat their patients, and often have a positive stake in more procedures. Rare is the hospital that routinely reviews the costs generated for the same DRG across physicians, questioning the decision processes used by physicians who are consistent outliers. This absence of accountability has stimulated a tendency to test more, to treat more, and to consume more health services, with little, if any, incentive to save costs. Not surprisingly, costs have gone up without any necessary improvement in health outcomes.

The consumers who have had employer-based healthcare coverage also don't have any accountability for costs. They have no real line of sight to how increasing healthcare costs have negatively impacted their salary, so they don't even know that they should be participating in an informed way to make decisions that balance costs versus outcomes. As a result, they have no meaningful incentive to save costs.

If there were incentives for consumers to manage costs, including modifying their own health behaviors, they would demand much better cost and outcome information than the mortality and morbidity data in other words is still the provider industry norm. Imagine if the auto repair industry competed for customers on such a "mortality and morbidity" value proposition. Repair shops would run commercials advertising that "your car is less likely to never run again if you come to our garage," or "come see us because we're less likely to remove your engine when you come in for a simple oil change!"

A fundamental economic premise has been ignored in the creation of a payment system that has no accountability. When the product is highly desired and associated with real value, *demand curves always go up when the cost of the product is free* or close to that. The solution to payment reform will have to build in this currently lacking accountability across stakeholders if the corrective pressures of a free market are to be unleashed.

End of the Model Year

One of the realities thoroughly ignored by the Obama administration's healthcare reform efforts has been that the fundamental business model of healthcare is driving most of the problems in the system. What we mean by *business model* is the way in which healthcare providers are paid for what they do. It's called *fee-for-service*. In this model the hospital and physicians are essentially working on a time-and-materials basis—the more services they provide for a patient, the more they make. This, and the fact that consumers don't typically pay directly for their healthcare services, has largely contributed to overutilization and spiraling cost inflation, which has averaged 10% annually over the last decade.

The downsides of fee-for-service are not news. In fact, this country's largest payer, CMS, has attempted to deal with the problem for decades. In the early 1980s, CMS introduced a new way of paying for healthcare—DRGs. Rather than rely on the "usual and customary" payment method for services that *were* rendered, DRGs ushered in the concept of a fixed price for a defined bundle of services—a "prospective" payment in which highly efficient providers stood to make more on the service (e.g., hip replacement), and inefficient providers lost money. Unfortunately, CMS never connected prospective payment to outcomes, and, predictably, quality problems increased along with continuously rising costs.

Outside of healthcare reform legislation, CMS recently declared that it will no longer reimburse providers for so-called *never events* (e.g., falls, hospital-acquired infections, surgeries on the wrong site, and readmissions within 30 days for the same problem). This is clearly an attempt to connect activity and outcomes, another critical aspect of fundamental business model change.

Historically, hospitals have actually been paid to fix the mistakes they made! It's like taking your car to the auto repair shop for an oil change and winding up with a bill for a cracked engine block that occurred in the process. Not surprisingly, CMS's administrative change has triggered a new focus on safety. How bold it will be remains to be seen. Our perspective is that increasing awareness by consumers and employers followed by demands for transparency and predictability will be the real levers of change.

What's long been recognized in other industries is that quality and cost must be addressed together, and consumers need to have a line of sight to the value they receive to make informed choices. After 25 years, CMS has finally reached the same conclusion. CMS covers roughly half of all healthcare spending in the United States. As for the other 50% of healthcare, largely handled by private insurers, the path that CMS has laid down offers some cover. Given the intense level of public dissatisfaction with ongoing premium increases by commercial insurers, they have a vested interest in business model innovation in healthcare delivery that offers the potential to deliver better value. That's good news, because the current model is looking very, very dated.

Understanding Healthcare Reform as Business Model Change

Healthcare is big business. Despite the window dressing, when you get right down to creating change in any industry, it's all about the money—who pays, for what, and how. Economic incentives work in a very nuanced way, consciously and subconsciously, and drive decisions. This fact operates even in healthcare across *all* segments.

As you'll recall from Chapter 1, healthcare isn't the first industry to face the need for a fundamentally different business model. All industries go through periods of such transition as a result of significant changes in their regulatory environment, competition, technology, or market expectations. These times of transition are very difficult. They force *all* stakeholders to rethink their business models and challenge fundamental assumptions about their markets—who their customers are, what products and services they offer, and how best to bring them to market.

Rethinking a business model requires a transfusion of fresh thinking, and that requires an *external analysis* of customers—in this case, healthcare consumers and a network of influencers, including payers and providers—to identify *truly unmet needs*. Such analysis, if it's going to be successful, must go well beyond what is understood as traditional market research, which is typically constrained in its design to dimension potential demand for services as *they are defined today.* For example, hospitals study the demographics of the population in the geographic area they serve and project demand accordingly. The real unmet need that's ignored in this approach is the fact that most people don't want to go to a hospital. As one hospital executive put it, "If we're really providing health*care*, we're putting ourselves out of business as we have traditionally known it."

Underlying the development of a new business model is the need to identify a better value proposition. The health-care industry has historically been focused on a *clinical* value proposition. New drugs and devices must meet efficacy and safety standards to get approved. The lengthy approval process, governed by the Food and Drug Administration (FDA), follows very specific research requirements that demand significant evidence that a given product works for a specific population and causes no harm (i.e., it's safe and efficacious). Health outcomes in the hospital setting, for the most part, have historically only been measured in terms of gross mortality and morbidity rates associated with given procedures. The industry has experienced a surge of innovation, providing more and better treatment options, but at increasingly higher costs. Now costs have reached an unsustainable level. Missing in the current fee-for-service payment method, which assigns an economic value procedure by procedure, is any analysis of *total economic and clinical value* over a continuum of care. This is the essence of trying to achieve better outcomes at lower cost—which should be the ultimate objective of any attempt at healthcare reform.

Once unmet needs and new economic and clinical value propositions are identified, they must be operationalized. Creating a new business model requires developing new *infrastructure*—defining new mandates for core functions and developing new capabilities and supporting processes. This is enormously hard work and, not surprisingly, it typically meets with great resistance. Reform efforts have usually recognized this potential resistance and have attempted to structure work to include all stakeholders in some type of business model redesign. The problem is that each stakeholder comes to the party to protect their own interests first. Change is fine, as long as it happens to someone else! And, without an overarching integrated strategic approach to the problem—in other words, a new design—reform efforts are doomed to tweak "what is" at the margins, with horse trading the norm and no real change the unfortunate result.

Effective new business model implementation requires an integrated approach that brings to the surface and resolves sources of resistance as well as unintended consequences. Every segment of the industry—from pharma, to device and diagnostics manufacturers, to payers, providers, employers, and consumers—will need to come to terms with the fundamental changes that will be required, or we face the real possibility of destroying what works in the industry and going broke in the process.

Central Role of Payment Reform

There is increasing awareness that the healthcare financing mechanisms in place today do not align with the goals of disease prevention, improved health outcomes, and reduced costs.[2] Changing these mechanisms starts with different and better answers to four key questions:

1. Who pays?
2. How does the payment exchange occur?
3. What gets paid for?
4. And, at the end of the day, is it worth it? (Are we getting value for what's delivered?)

The answers to these questions must take a systematic approach that considers the agendas of, and impact on, all stakeholders, including payers, providers, manufacturers, employers, government, and consumers. Ultimately, each of these segments must make changes in an orchestrated, coordinated, and integrated manner, or the changes won't be effective.

Whenever change is introduced, there are *always* unanticipated and unintended consequences. Uncoordinated "islands" or "siloed" approaches to change increase the likelihood of such unintended consequences. As change is introduced in one area, there are ripple effects as the change begins to impact other areas. There are two examples that clearly illustrate this point, and they are central to understanding the healthcare fix we're in today.

Unintended Consequences: The Hospital Example

Paying for Volume, Not Results

Hospitals today are paid on a production basis reflecting what they *do* to people. There is no incentive to keep people out of the hospital. They are only paid when people are admitted to the hospital. Increasing volume is good in this business model. The more patients and the more procedures, the more they make. Hospitals are clearly in the *sickness* business, not the prevention or wellness business. As one hospital CFO said, "I'm not investing one dime in wellness—it doesn't pay the bills. And I don't think it ever will!" Coming from an acute care, sickness business model, he can't conceive of anything else. So success for hospitals has meant more procedures. Since someone else was paying, a third-party insurer or employer in most cases, increasing costs didn't really matter—until recently.

Real Impact of CMS on Quality of Care and Costs

It's ironic that the first time the healthcare delivery industry took costs seriously was when CMS introduced DRGs as an alternative to the traditional retrospective method of usual and customary rate (UCR) payment. This was a well-intended attempt to impose cost controls in a situation that CMS recognized more than thirty years ago wasn't sustainable.

Hospitals were given incentives to improve their *efficiency*, since any difference between their actual costs and their DRG reimbursement was *profit* or *loss*. Few anticipated that the way in which they would choose to lower costs would result in many of the serious quality issues and increased costs we face today. Hospitals created a *production environment* focused on increasing demand and capacity to handle more procedures to offset lower revenues per procedure. Investments in new technology, like imaging equipment, for example, have added pressure to make these purchases pay for themselves. Combined with consumer interest in having the latest test (especially when a third party pays), limited awareness of their associated risks, and providers' reliance on technology to offset perceived threats of malpractice, there have been steady pressures to build volume. As a result, many hospital executives in private conversations estimate that 30–40% of the "care" delivered today isn't clinically necessary! And these estimates are from people managing some of our nation's best institutions.

CMS's introduction of DRGs as a means to control costs was based on an assumption that hospitals would *ensure quality* as part of any change. Unfortunately, that hasn't proven to be the case, a point we predicted at the time. As noted in the cover story of the September 2009 issue of *Consumer Reports*,[3] hospitals aren't as safe or as sanitary as they should be— something insiders have known for years. In a side-by-side survey of nurses and patients, two very different perspectives emerged:

- 28% of nurses saw problems with hospital cleanliness, while only 4% of patients saw problems;
- 38% of nurses said that care wasn't coordinated properly compared to 13% of patients;
- 26% of nurses said that hospital staff sometimes didn't wash their hands, while only 5% of patients observed this.

In their efforts to cut costs, during the late 1980s and 1990s many hospitals partially dismantled the infrastructure they needed to ensure quality. They slashed the ranks of first-line and middle management, seriously compromising their capability to build, monitor, and correct quality processes as an inherent part of doing the work. As a result, an *unintended consequence* of CMS's effort to control costs is that consumers now face a significant risk of getting sicker in a hospital rather than better.

This unintended consequence of the DRG approach to cost control has more recently led to yet another band-aid. CMS has informed the industry that it will no longer pay for so-called "never events"—medical problems that the hospital created or should have avoided, such as hospital-acquired infections, medication errors, or falls. Putting responsibility back on hospitals for fixing their mistakes is a belated attempt to reconnect cost and quality—something that was decoupled by CMS when DRGs were first introduced.

The premise is that if hospitals are responsible for paying for their errors, they'll make sure that errors are prevented. What's now being discussed is the idea of refusing to pay for 30-day readmissions for the same diagnosis. The intent is to force better discharge planning and coordination with community services, which was once the service hallmark of many healthcare delivery organizations under usual and customary rates, but not cost effective under DRGs.

Imagine buying a new flatscreen television and being expected to pay to fix the manufacturer's quality problems! Not surprisingly, one of the most transformative actions in recent years has been CMS's decision NOT to reimburse providers for the so-called never events noted above. And, it didn't require an act of Congress to create the change. If the basic rule of *follow the money* was actually followed, we'd see that payers' propensity to pay for volume without regard to quality drives volume without regard to quality.

Lost in this series of CMS band-aids is the fact that healthcare payment is mired in minutiae that in and of itself is contributing to the cost problem. The implementation of DRGs was a cost-accounting approach that has actually spawned a whole new industry to help providers figure it out in order to get paid. Care providers spend a considerable amount of time coding their interventions for maximum reimbursement, time which could be spent with patients. In addition to introducing a complexity that has significantly increased administrative costs, this payment method has also completely disconnected payment from outcomes, which is what the money is supposed to be achieving in the first place. A subindustry devoted to maximizing reimbursement per case has also been spawned as providers learn to upcode in an effort to maintain revenue—life support for a dying business model.

The unanticipated consequences of DRGs illustrate what can happen when changes are introduced as isolated actions rather than as a series of integrated steps across stakeholders. Instead of controlling costs, this change in payment has triggered additional administrative costs, a deluge of unnecessary care, and an erosion of quality of care—all unintended consequences that have significantly added to the costs of healthcare rather than reducing them.

Unintended Consequences: The Primary Care Example

Consider the circumstances of an independent primary care doctor we recently interviewed. He's an internist who takes great pride in his ability to help his patients manage their chronic diseases—asthma, diabetes, various cardiac problems, and so on. The more complicated the case, the more he gets to serve as "medical detective." His patients appreciate him because of his thoroughness, and because he so effectively diagnoses and helps them manage their conditions, in contrast to their previous physician experiences. As a result, they maximize their quality of life, avoiding complications, unnecessary hospital visits, and multitudes of specialists.

He takes the time to ask questions and diagnose the root cause(s) behind his patients' symptoms, utilizing expensive diagnostic tests only when necessary. He uses visits to educate his patients, guiding them to better manage their health to avoid preventable healthcare interventions if their condition progresses. He coordinates care among needed specialists to whom he refers his patients when he has determined that he really needs their consultation.

Discouraging the Type of Care That Results in Better Outcomes

Unfortunately, he's penalized in our current payment system, yet his behavior is exactly what's needed to lower costs and improve outcomes! His time to educate patients isn't reimbursed. Or, if he codes for an extended visit to recoup his legitimate time spent, his claim is much more likely to be flagged by an insurer as an outlier and will either be rejected outright or result in delayed payment. Unfortunately, his behavior is not typical of primary care today. It's a much easier path for the primary care doctor to pass his patient on to a specialist, reducing his liability, and in the process, increasing costs to the system.

Once again, approaching the work of primary care physicians on a piecework basis has resulted in the unintended consequences of both increased costs and reduced quality. To sustain a viable income, primary care physicians have focused on maximizing the number of patients they see rather than spending the amount of time necessary to guide their patients and orchestrate their necessary care. As a result, more expensive specialists are utilized unnecessarily. Care is fragmented and uncoordinated between doctors, increasing the likelihood of errors and the redundant use of expensive tests.

Creating a Critical Shortage of the "Right" Kind of Doctors

Beyond the negative cost and quality impacts of the way we're paying primary care physicians is an even larger problem. Just as we're realizing the critical importance of primary care to achieve improved outcomes at lower costs, we're facing a severe shortage of primary care physicians. Why does this shortage exist, and why is it currently projected to get worse? Quite simply, the answer is financial. There is little incentive today for graduating medical students to choose careers in primary care specialties. Since primary care doctors are the lowest paid of all physicians, graduating medical students with hundreds of thousands of dollars of school loans are choosing primary care specialties with much lower frequency. Only 14% of internal medicine residency graduates choose to stay in general internal medicine. The rest opt for the more lucrative subspecialties in which they are paid to do procedures such as cardiac catheterization and endoscopies. Medicare and insurance companies pay much more for procedures than the intellectual capability of primary care physicians to diagnose, provide, and coordinate care, which can often obviate the need for expensive procedures.

As noted by the Center for Payment Reform, "payments should create market incentives that foster an adequate supply of clinicians to meet the needs of an aging population and to ensure that all patients have access to high quality and afford-able healthcare services. ... Creating market incentives will require more highly valuing primary care functions related to evaluation, counseling and coordination relative to the value of procedural, diagnostic, and interventional care."

Healthcare Is *Big* Business

The hospital and primary care physician compensation exam-ples just described illustrate the failure of uncoordinated, isolated efforts to make improvements and the unintended negative consequences they bring. Any realistic effort to create an improved business model for healthcare must comprehen-sively address the extraordinarily complex array of multiple stakeholders involved, as illustrated in Figure 2.1.

Successful business model change must anticipate and plan for the fact that each of the stakeholders in Figure 2.1 has an agenda, and a vested interest in maximizing it. In such a market environment, incentives must be aligned. Creating a new business model to improve care and reduce costs must be approached systemically, integrating changes across and within the parts so that the intended solutions work together.

Considering our current national economic situation and the level that healthcare costs have reached—estimated at approximately one sixth of Gross National Product (GNP)—it's understandable that many want to look for someone to blame. It's certainly politically expedient to single out private health-care insurers or drug and medical device manufacturers as pri-mary causes of our cost problem. But *looking for a scapegoat* (and forcing change only in that area) is the wrong answer

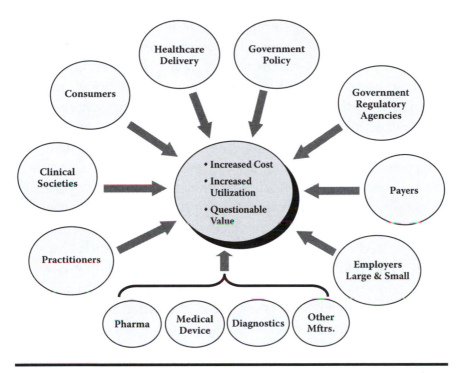

Figure 2.1 Healthcare stakeholder clusters. (Courtesy of Numerof & Associates, Inc.)

and would just repeat the isolated, band-aid approach to fixing the system that we've taken in the past.

Recent Example

Since the U.S. healthcare system has become so convoluted, piecemeal approaches to resolving the problem won't work and tend to exacerbate the situation. Here's a very recent example.

CMS is conducting the Acute Care Episode (ACE) Demonstration Project—a government-sponsored pilot effort that tests whether delivering certain medical services at a fixed price can yield cost savings without compromising quality. In the pilot, for example, orthopedic surgeons were encouraged to find ways to lower the cost of a typical knee replacement. One of the common solutions was to standardize on a more limited number of artificial knee joints than had typically been used.

This meant eliminating the highest-cost manufacturers of joints and working with a smaller selection of possible products.

The key motivator of this activity was that the surgeons were promised a check for some portion of the money saved. This is where the story gets interesting. The Department of Justice is actively pursuing investigations of manufacturers who did essentially the same thing. They said to surgeons, "use our products and we'll find a way to compensate you." Yet just because a surgeon held a patent on a product or spoke on behalf of the product didn't mean that the product wasn't optimal for the patient. In any case, the Department of Justice has collected millions of dollars in fines to settle such cases of alleged and real impropriety. The core principle is that personal gain by the physician shouldn't be allowed to bias their clinical decision. So why is it a great idea when CMS signs the check and a criminal offense when it's signed by a manufacturer? Someone's agenda always controls decisions that affect your healthcare.

Even in the absence of agendas by CMS or manufacturers, doctors under the current fee-for-service system generate more income when they provide more service. On the face of it, the scenario is no different from a patron in a restaurant—the more you order and the more expensive the meal is, the more the owner makes. The big difference is that at the restaurant, you know what you're ordering and you know what the cost will be. In healthcare you have no line of sight to the costs and limited information with which to evaluate the quality of what you're buying.

The real issue in the healthcare debate is what it will take to make your agenda count. No one is really talking about this.

Creating a Competitive, Functioning Market

Many voices in our current national debate are advising against too much government intervention and the preservation of a natural market. While this is directionally the right approach, it implies that a functioning market has been at work in the past. Nothing could be farther from the truth!

There Is Little Accountability in the Current System

As we noted at the beginning of the chapter, a functioning market requires accountability for the cost consequences of decisions. In the case of healthcare, these costs reflect the care decisions between physicians and their patients. Across the industry, this accountability is very hard to find and, unfortunately, more the exception than the rule. As we've described, providers and consumers are driving unnecessary utilization that in turn drives unnecessary costs. Quality has slipped but providers have been compensated for fixing the problems they've created. And private insurers have followed CMS's lead in lockstep to create a payment system that encourages over-utilization rather than quality and cost control.

As our hospital and primary care physician examples illustrated, when we remove accountability for the consequences of our actions, we realize unintended negative consequences. Any solution to payment reform will have to build in this currently lacking accountability *across* stakeholders if the corrective pressures of a natural, competitive market are to be unleashed.

There Is Little Information Available on Which to Base Responsible Care Decisions

Assuming consumers had incentives to manage costs, including modifying their own health behaviors, they would demand much better information than the mortality and morbidity outcome data in other words is typically available.

As the Health Quality Alliance steering committee noted, it's hard to tell which providers are doing a good job and which aren't.[4] They, too, recognize that in contrast to most well-functioning markets, there is a lack of consistent information about our fragmented healthcare system that can be used to improve outcomes while keeping costs down. They argue for a "nationally consistent, technologically sound, and efficient approach to make performance information widely available," recognizing that under no circumstances can you improve something you can't measure.

Our bias is that clinical societies, in concert with others, have the opportunity *and* responsibility to define performance measures for routine, predictable procedures. We will have to be more cautious and flexible with complex situations, where diagnosis is difficult and disagreements on courses of care can be expected. There is danger in formulaic approaches to all care needs, but this should not preclude establishing standards for more routine, predictable care.

Another critical requirement of a free market is an industry's ability to self-monitor and correct. To this point, the healthcare delivery industry has demonstrated an inability to do this. When hospitals had the money to invest in information technology in order to improve efficiency and effectiveness, they didn't do it. Now the industry is playing catch-up with a government mandate to implement electronic medical records.

Providers have historically just passed increasing costs on to payers, rather than cultivate a culture focused on continuous efficiency improvement—until payers pushed back. But the pushback wasn't a collaborative effort to determine new approaches to care that were more effective and efficient. It was just the dictate of an arbitrary discounted price like any buyer with muscle pushes on its suppliers.

And consumers, encouraged by their employers and insurers long ago, now have a warped sense of entitlement, viewing healthcare insurance as free unlimited care rather than protection against catastrophic financial costs. The solution to payment reform must make the necessary information available and align incentives for all stakeholders to self-monitor, make decisions, and act accordingly.

There Is Already Enough Money in the System

Part of our national debate on healthcare reform is whether or not we can afford it. In fact, it's possible to ensure coverage for all without increasing cost, without increasing taxes, without creating increased debt, and without introducing yet another government solution.

Based on a report from UnitedHealth Group's Center for Health Reform and Modernization, "the federal government could save $540 billion in healthcare costs over the next 10 years *if existing, proven programs* and techniques that have improved healthcare quality and slowed the growth of medical spending *are applied more broadly* ..."[5,6] (emphasis added).

A broader look at the entire industry promises even greater savings potential if common errors and unnecessary services can be reduced. With the proper incentives, we've estimated that we can easily find $500 billion annually that we're unnecessarily spending. For starters:

■ According to the Agency for Healthcare Research and Quality (AHRQ), medication errors cost $5.6 million per hospital annually. Across 5,000 hospitals, that represents *$28 billion* of annual unnecessary cost. (In a recent *American Hospital Association* (AHA) News article, one hospital was praised for reducing medication errors from 20% to 8%, ignoring the larger question of how an 8% error rate was acceptable in the first place!)[7]

■ Projects to reduce length of stay (LOS) at top hospitals in areas of medicine conservatively estimated an annual cost of $75 million per hospital for unnecessary LOS. Considering there are over 5,000 hospitals in the United States,[8] *better care coordination* and corresponding *reduction in LOS* can easily produce $380 billion in annual savings.

■ Leading hospital executives estimate that 30–40% of the care they are providing is *clinically unnecessary.* Considering over $650 billion of care is annually provided by hospitals,[9] eliminating 15% of that care (vs. 30–40%) represents an annual savings of *$100 billion.*

The United States already spends more money on healthcare than other developed countries on a per capita basis, so spending even more on top of that defies basic logic! *The problem isn't that we're not spending enough; it's that we're not spending it appropriately.* As we've illustrated, there is at least $500 billion per year that can be redeployed. And this is before we deal with the fraud and abuse in the system.

There Is a Solution, and It's Closer than Some Think

In the process of creating the real change we all desire from healthcare reform, we need to be *really clear* about *what* we're changing and *why*, and what the impacts are likely to be, both intended and unintended. If we introduce change, but we don't address the underlying causes of inefficiency, duplication, and error, we won't solve the problem!

This will require a yet-to-be-developed, integrated strategy and corresponding set of solutions that rest on an understanding of the drivers of our current problems. This integrated strategy must effectively align and implement change across all stakeholders. Isolated band-aids haven't fixed anything and have actually exacerbated the problem. Successful reform will require the planned and coordinated creation of a fundamentally new business model for healthcare that aligns the financing mechanisms of the industry with the goals of prevention, improved quality, and reduced costs.

There is an important role for government in this new business model creation, but it isn't legislating the new model. We need legislation to enable more healthcare insurance competition. By mandating that all insurance policies provide a common set of coverage ("Essential Health Benefits"), the current legislation requires everyone to have comprehensive, highly controversial, and costly insurance. Regardless of whether or not the US Supreme Court upholds the mandate, insurance companies can design and offer solutions to meet the myriad needs within the construct of a truly American solution. And we have enough money in the current system to cover Americans without insurance. Government doesn't need to raise more money with new taxes or go into more debt.

Finally, we need to make certain that consumers are at the center of our new business model. They need to have meaningful outcome information in order to make good cost–benefit choices and ensure they are receiving real economic and clinical value. And they wouldn't have to be dependent on their employers for insurance if we eliminate barriers in healthcare insurance and create a truly competitive market space.

Endnotes

1. "Practical Strategies for Healthcare Reform" by Rita E. Numerof, *Medical Progress Today*, November 13, 2009, http://www.medicalprogresstoday.com/spotlight/spotlight_indarchive.php?id=1830.
2. "Healthcare Reform: Strategy, Myths and Solutions" by Rita E. Numerof, *Medical Progress Today*, November 13, 2009, http://www.medicalprogresstoday.com/spotlight/spotlight_indarchive.php?id=1830.

3. "Patients, Beware: 731 Nurses Reveal What to Watch Out for in the Hospital," September 2009. *Consumer Reports*, http://www.consumerreports.org/health/doctors-hospitals/hospitals/overview/hospitals-and-nurses-ov.htm.

4. Quality Alliance Steering Committee, "Charting the Course to High-Value Health Care," March 2009, http://www.healthqualityalliance.org/userfiles/HVHC%20Issue%20Brief%20Final.pdf.

5. Center for Payment Reform, "Payment Reform Principles," April 2009, www.centerforpayment.org.

6. UnitedHealth Group. *Federal Health Care Cost Containment: How in Practice Can it Be Done?* Working Paper 1, May 2009, http://www.unitedhealthgroup.com/hrm/UNH_WorkingPaper1.pdf.

7. UnitedHealth Group. "UnitedHealth Group Identifies More than $500 Billion in Specific Health Care Costs Savings to the Federal Government Over the Next 10 Years," May 27, 2009, http://www.unitedhealthgroup.com/main/Newsroom.aspx.

8. Jennifer Towne, "Hospitals In Pursuit of Excellence: One Hospital's Path to Improving Medication Safety," August 31, 2009, *AHA News*.

9. American Hospital Statistics, *2009 Profile of U.S. Community Hospitals*, http://www.ahadata.com/ahadata/html/WallChart.html.

Chapter 3

In the Eye of the Storm: The Role of Consumers and Employers

When consumers hear about healthcare reform, they ask three questions: Why should I care? What am I going to lose? What's in it for me? As much of the current healthcare debate has focused on changes to systems and processes, it doesn't translate well to the individual, so consumers typically aren't interested in following the debate. Yet, when changes are discussed, consumers become concerned with what they may lose and automatically assume that any changes will be a detriment to them. When they're presented with new options, like high-deductible health plans (HDHPs) and health savings accounts (HSAs), consumers want to know what the benefit of engaging in these new models will be and how it will affect their current state.

Regardless of the situation, consumers know that they need information in order to make good choices. But they run into some interesting problems in the process.

It is extraordinarily difficult for consumers to get information about cost, quality, and outcomes in healthcare as the necessary information isn't readily available. Even after they've undergone a procedure and are looking at the explanation of benefits sent by their insurer, they aren't always sure what services they received, how much those services really cost, or what if anything they owe!

And when consumers do ask questions, the questions aren't universally welcomed by providers. This could be a result of the providers not having information because *they* don't know what the true costs of care are. And why is this? It's because cost hasn't mattered since someone else always pays the bill. As a result, critical discussions about cost, quality, and outcomes that should take place between physicians and patients don't.

A Personal Example

One of us recently encountered an experience that drove this last point home. Michael had a small lump in the palm of his hand that occasionally became tender. The internist, after feeling around without insight, recommended a hand surgeon. At the appointment three weeks later, the hand surgeon did the same "feel around," reiterated the obvious ("you have some kind of mass"), and recommended an x-ray, conveniently located on the premises. Michael's not a clinician, but even he knows that x-rays don't adequately show soft tissue, which this mass surely was. But he followed the doctor's instruction and had the x-ray.

To no one's surprise, the x-ray was uninformative. "It's almost certainly benign, but I need more information before I can tell you what it is." The surgeon suggested that Michael get an MRI at the hospital's outpatient radiology department, "because it's convenient and the results come up on this screen, right here." Two weeks later, Michael was filling in the same paperwork he'd filled in for the surgeon (how "convenient") when he read the small print that said the MRI would cost a minimum of $1,300, possibly more. He gagged.

That's when he realized several things. First, that he didn't care that much about a condition that was a minor irritant. And second, that whatever it was, the next conversation with the surgeon (after the charge for interpretation of the MRI) would likely go like this:

Surgeon: "Well Michael, it looks like a [your choice of technical term]," or "I'm still not clear about what you've got there, but whatever it is, I could cut it out, assuming that's what you want me to do. Recognize that no surgery is without risk. So the question for you to decide is how troubling this is and whether it's worth it for you to undergo surgery."

Since Michael already knew the answer to that last question, he left the imaging center, vowing to ask better questions at the start.

Michael realized that he hadn't asked what difference the MRI would make when it was recommended. If he'd been talking to an auto repair shop and they recommended a $1,300 test, he would have asked that question. We've all been conditioned to accept physician recommendations without much examination. Michael's HSA-mediated consumer experience prompted him (better late than never) to ask why: Why do I need this? What will be learned? How will it make a difference?

The operative assumption behind our easy acceptance of physician recommendations is that they're always in our best interest. With the many changes going on in healthcare, there are too many other potential agendas out there to count on that any more. As patients, we need to approach the purchase of healthcare services in the same way that we purchase any other service, whether we have an HSA or not.

When it comes to healthcare, we need to stop thinking like patients and act more like consumers. That's not always easy. When we're at a physician's office, we often find ourselves dressed in a paper gown that barely covers us, stripped of our identities and dignity for our "well-being." Being dressed like this creates a feeling of vulnerability and helplessness, with a desire to get back to our street clothes as quickly as possible.

When the physician comes in, we seldom ask questions and accept the diagnosis and treatment with minimal discussion. If they haven't already collected it, we pay our copay and leave. But when we're in the market for a new television or automobile or even insurance—important and expensive purchases—we become consumers. We ask lots of questions about product features and benefits, comparison shop for the best value for our money, and negotiate payment terms to get the best deal. So why don't we universally apply these same skills to healthcare in decisions regarding our most precious possession—our health?

As the example shows, consumers in most other markets make their decisions with their wallets and their feet.

At a spring 2012 program sponsored by The Heritage Foundation, Senator Tom Coburn, a physician from Oklahoma, described an exception to this behavior. He believes that the Amish in his community are the best purchasers of healthcare and provided compelling examples to illustrate his point. The Amish don't have health insurance. And when they seek medical help, they ask for a list of all anticipated costs. They ask lots of questions about the *need* for a given treatment or procedure, and they look for the provider willing to give them the best price. Once a decision to move forward is made, they actively and respectfully negotiate deals and ask questions like, "If I pay in advance, do I get a discount?" From our perspective, this should be normative.

Whose Agenda Controls Your Healthcare? Another Look

One of the hotly debated issues that continues to surface *and resurface* is the question about conflict-of-interest concerns when it comes to physicians and their relationship to manufacturers and specific products. In a nutshell, critics argue that physicians should have no monetary relationship to the products they use, recommend, or prescribe in the treatment of their patients. Their only concern should be their patient's well-being, and a financial tie to testing or products puts that focus at risk. Taken at face value, this seems like a reasonable position. But is it?

Imagine an experienced orthopedic surgeon who decides he has a better idea for a surgical implant in the treatment of lower back pain, especially degenerative disk disorder, than what's on the market. He builds a prototype, gets a patent, and takes it to a manufacturer who likes the concept, agrees to invest in clinical trials, and successfully commercializes the product. The manufacturer has a royalty agreement with the physician-inventor and both parties make a lot of money as the market realizes the superior value of the product based on legitimate, objective outcome data. So what's the problem? If the inventor believes in his product line and thinks it's in the best interest of his patients to use it, why should he be penalized for using it, and since he invented it, why shouldn't he be compensated for it? Based on some policy positions this isn't a good thing.

To illustrate the point, let's walk through an analogy. Imagine you're in the market for a device that allows you to listen to all your favorite music anywhere without bothering anyone else around you. After talking to your friends, doing some research on the net, and looking at product ratings, you approach—you guessed it—the local Apple store in your favorite mall. Apple sells its products in Apple stores; it doesn't offer consumers brand choice (i.e., Apple vs. non-Apple) but it has a deep product line to meet lots of diverse consumer needs. The consumer shops, gathers information, and makes the decision to buy the Apple product. The consumer makes the judgment on the perceived value of the product—its features and benefits—and not on the basic components in the device.

Clearly, deciding to have surgery, picking the surgeon to perform the operation, and determining what product to use are fundamentally more consequential than deciding to buy an iPod. But there's an interesting parallel. The informed health-care consumer gets referrals, checks available data, talks to the surgeon candidates, gets second or third opinions, explores outcomes, and lands on a decision, ultimately placing their most important possession, their life, in the hands of that surgeon—extending trust.

Shouldn't the surgeon who is responsible for protecting that trust have the freedom, without legislative barriers influencing (and coloring) their clinical judgment, to determine which products will work best for this patient? To do anything less would represent interference of the state in the private matter between physician and patient. So if the surgeon invented the product, believes in it, and uses it, why shouldn't he be entitled to his royalty stream? If he's transparent about the relationship to the product and the patient has done his due diligence in selecting the surgeon, couldn't this also increase the patient's trust/confidence in the outcome?

Let's take this one step further. Let's assume that the surgeon isn't the inventor, but she trained on the product line, trusts the "tools," and believes in the product. Not surprisingly, the manufacturer reaches out, maybe engages the surgeon in clinical studies, and asks her to do some workshops on behalf of the line. The manufacturer compensates the surgeon, using a defensible fair market value (FMV) fee. And the problem with this is? Does the federal government think it wise to tell physicians you can either practice medicine or you can invent; you just can't do both? We don't think so. Having said this, there is a role for government.

Realistically, there are unscrupulous surgeons just as there are unscrupulous individuals and shady characters in every profession and every walk of life. This isn't a new problem; it's been around for thousands of years. Thinking we can legislate trust and integrity or eliminate greed with a law is delusional. And at the end of the day, this is really what it's about: trust, integrity, and greed.

You earn the first; you either have integrity or you don't. Dishonesty, fraud, abuse—often a reflection of unbridled greed and arrogance—can be tempered, and legislation can play a role in this—it can make information available to enable good decisions, recognizing they will always be imperfect. Efforts to report outcomes and increasing focus on transparency in healthcare will enable consumers and independent groups to make informed choices.

You pick the doctor and let the doctor pick the tools that will be best for you, but make sure the evidence on which that choice is made passes the proverbial smell test.

Perversion of the Concept of Insurance

Too often in the debate about healthcare reform there is no distinction between saying that Americans have *no healthcare* versus saying they have *no health insurance*. We've reached a point where the method of financing healthcare has become synonymous with the care itself.

The need for insurance is obvious. It protects us from catastrophic financial expenses. That's why we buy car insurance, home insurance, life insurance, and personal liability insurance. Certainly there is a parallel need for health insurance, considering that we one day may require urgent, extensive care that would cost far more than the average person could expect to finance. So, some form of catastrophic coverage makes good personal business sense.

However, health insurance has become different from other types of insurance. For the most part, we have begun to use health insurance to pay for almost all health-related expenses, not just the catastrophic ones. We expect it to cover regular checkups or an antibiotic prescription for a standard sinus infection. If other insurance worked the same way, we'd expect our auto insurance to pay for oil changes, or our homeowners insurance to pay the plumber to unclog a toilet. If this actually happened, auto and home insurance would cost much more than they do today. To make matters worse, we've become used to someone else (i.e., employers or government) footing the bill, and have largely become bystanders in the process.

Where Do Employers Fit into the Equation?

So where does business fit into the picture? We are on the cusp of a fundamental change in the business model of healthcare. The industry has reached a tipping point, which is creating changes in the way we pay for and deliver healthcare. As we outline in the following chapters, we clearly can't continue to do what we've been doing—or we'll go broke doing it!

Business leaders have an opportunity *and a responsibility* to influence change to ensure that their employees get better health, better outcomes, and greater value. Think about it— businesses pay directly for care in that they write the checks for healthcare insurance—and those checks are getting bigger. Businesses also pay indirectly for healthcare due to absentee-ism and presenteeism (those who are distracted at the work-place due to health issues and have decreased productivity as a result). Historically, when businesses have tried to influence change in the healthcare model, it's been in the context of the current model. Employers would pressure insurance compa-nies to lower costs, add wellness programs, engage Pharmacy Benefit Managers (PBMs) to move pharmaceutical products to generic drugs, and offer HDHPs. But these efforts haven't worked! It's time to move back toward the original role of insur-ance—providing a safety net for catastrophic circumstances.

What Can Consumers and Employers Do?

Going forward, employees and employers can have a very pow-erful voice. There are a few simple steps these groups can take.

Demand Transparency and Accountability

At a bare minimum, patients should think of themselves as consumers. They should know *what* they're getting and what the associated costs are. But to make a good decision as to whether or not the treatment is necessary, consumers need more line of sight to outcomes. They should be able to have a dialogue with their healthcare providers about the variety of treatments available to them, the potential outcomes associated with each option, and their related risks and costs. Accepting the physician's word isn't sufficient; consumers must ask for evidence to support the recommendations so they can gauge the likelihood of the potential outcomes proposed—and that evidence needs to be conveyed in consumer-friendly terms by a clinician you trust.

Employers are in a position to demand transparency and accountability for outcomes on behalf of their employees. Increasingly, these progressive employers are intentionally selecting providers who demonstrate true transparency and accountability.

Move Conversation toward a Continuum of Care

Currently, most people only see a physician or other health-care providers when they have a problem. Consumers need to move away from these narrow acute episodes and move toward prevention. Cerner Corporation has committed resources to improve the health status of its employees. Building off its success internally, it's taken the approach to the broader Kansas City market, home to its corporate head-quarters. Community health competitions have resulted in weight loss and better health management.

Employers can also use their market clout to force change and reward innovation by demanding bundled, transparent pricing in other words tied to outcomes. Doing so will give them greater line of sight to their costs and help them to anticipate what their costs will be. Companies like Boeing and Lowe's have already begun to move in this direction.

Create/Become Informed Consumers

Businesses can help create informed consumers among employees and within their communities by demanding that insurers provide them with information that's easy for their employees to understand. Like any other market, different providers will offer what appears to be the same service at different costs. Employees need information to understand what their options are and the trade-offs for selecting among them. And employees need to hold their employers accountable for getting this information for them.

Create Incentives for Better Health Behaviors

Employers who offer insurance coverage to their employees can also adopt policies that promote accountability for good health choices and attempts to deter problematic behavior. As an example, Johnson & Johnson's corporate policy clearly discourages smoking. Any employee who wants to engage in tobacco use must go off property to do so. Sometimes, this means getting in your car and driving away. Johnson & Johnson also provides financial incentives for employees to participate in annual health screenings by paying them for completing a health assessment and additionally structures monetary rewards for health maintenance and improvement. A November 16, 2011 *New York Times* article by Reed Abelson highlights financial penalties some employers are placing on employees who smoke and are therefore expected to utilize as much as 25% more healthcare than nonsmokers. At companies like Home Depot, PepsiCo, and Walmart, cost differentials for smokers range from an additional $240 per year to $2000 per year more than nonsmokers.

Employers can also encourage employees to take an active role in managing their health expenses by moving to defined contribution plans as opposed to traditional defined benefit plans. A defined contribution consists of a fixed amount of money provided by the employer to the employee for the purchase of insurance that best meets his or her needs.

Change Is Never Easy, but It Is Possible

The challenge of creating informed, accountable consumers should not be underestimated. The healthcare delivery industry struggles to compare the *value* associated with treating at one hospital versus another, focusing primarily on costs *without adequate attention to differential outcomes* and the value associated with care that may be delivered under different cost structures *and* different clinical models.

As we'll discuss throughout this book, it's not *just* about lowering costs—it's about demonstrating economic *and* clinical value. And it's not just about the delivery and insurance sectors. It's about a *fundamentally different model* for the entire industry with a different equation that offers consumers real choice. And it offers our country a pathway to better healthcare and increased competitiveness.

Chapter 4

Comparative Effectiveness Research: Creating an Environment for Change

Until recently, *comparative effectiveness* was a term that only surfaced in conversations among health policy specialists, academicians, and other observers of the healthcare marketplace. No longer. The allocation of $1.1 billion to comparative effectiveness research (CER) in the American Recovery and Reinvestment Act (ARRA) of 2009 represented a paradigm shift. It promises to radically alter the level of government involvement in the way healthcare products and services are developed, delivered, and paid for. For better or worse, we believe this is a fact.[1]

The United States is a laggard in this arena. Other developed countries, including Britain, Canada, Germany, Australia, France, and the Netherlands, have all established infrastructures to serve the same general purpose, and for the same reason—they couldn't afford not to. Rapidly aging populations, coupled with rapid advances in technology and aggressive commercialization by manufacturers, made continued ad hoc decision making by providers economically untenable.

That's where the United States finds itself now. With health-care expenditures at almost 18% of gross domestic product (GDP),[2] our per capita expense is already more than 40% higher than other developed countries, and to make matters worse, our outcome metrics lag peers substantially. In this context, comparative effectiveness has emerged as a part of the broader challenge of healthcare reform.

Historically, decision making regarding the treatment of choice in a particular case has been the province of the attending physician in consultation with the patient. In situations where the treatment will be paid for by an insurer, which accounts for the overwhelming majority, the prime consideration has been anticipated clinical effectiveness. It's been the physician's role to weigh research and claims made by the manufacturer (subject to Food and Drug Administration [FDA] verification) and by academic and government-sponsored research.

Comparative effectiveness, at least as conceptualized in the ARRA, means more than that. Such research is explicitly mandated to take clinical effectiveness and (for all practical purposes) cost into consideration. And although the legislation implies that research results will be advisory in nature, given the broader economic context, it's hard to imagine such an effort culminating in such an outcome.

We believe a broad range of constituents with a stake in the healthcare marketplace needs to understand this initiative and what it's likely to mean to them.

Drivers of CER

Role of Cost Containment

The most basic impulse behind CER is the desire to control healthcare costs—an inescapable imperative if CMS's Medicare and Medicaid programs are to be saved from insolvency without dramatic tax increases.

The federal government currently spends more than 6.5% of GDP on healthcare through CMS, an amount that already exceeds the payroll taxes intended to pay for it. If costs continue to grow at their current pace, everyone else will have to pay out of pocket while simultaneously footing the bill for CMS.

There are a number of additional factors that have increased the pressure on CMS's budget. Wage growth was relatively slow in the years preceding the recession. Coupled with sustained unemployment, we have a smaller base from which to collect payroll taxes. Ironically, wage growth was slow, in part, because increasingly expensive medical benefits have displaced wages in total compensation. Another pressure stems from the fact that many unemployed have lost their health benefits, increasingly relying on the government for their care.

This combination of factors is recognized by policymakers as a long-term threat to the public health insurance system, and every major review of the status of the system recognizes the need to reduce costs, and the growth of costs, immediately and dramatically.

Ideally, policymakers would like to reduce costs without impacting the quality of healthcare, and CER is seen as one way to get there. By replacing ineffective treatments and standards of clinical care with effective ones, or by replacing more expensive treatments with equally effective, but less expensive ones, the cost of care can be brought down, in the words of the Congressional Budget Office (CBO), "without adverse health consequences."

The CBO has consistently pointed to evidence in support of the idea that there are massive savings to be had by changing patterns of clinical practice. The evidence for this comes from several sources. First, other countries have equivalent or better outcomes with much lower costs. Second, an analysis of Medicare spending showed large variations across regions in cost per patient that were not associated with increased illness, higher payment rates, or better outcomes. By some estimates, total Medicare costs could be reduced by 30% if the entire country adopted the clinical practice patterns of the most efficient regions. It has also been estimated that between 30% and 65% of all surgeries that are performed in high-use regions are either clinically inappropriate or of "equivocal" value.

Data like these have raised hopes on the part of politicians that, if only they knew what worked, they could drastically reduce the costs of care while retaining its quality. *What works* is the focus of CER.

Role of Political Expediency

It isn't all about politics, but politics will make itself felt. While CER certainly offers a legitimate, if partial, solution to the real problem of cost containment, it also plays off the perception that pharmaceutical and medical device companies have managed to game the system to extract exorbitant profits, artificially raising the cost of healthcare for everyone.

This perception has been largely created by the very real costs of patented drugs paid by American consumers and the much lower prices of these same drugs overseas. It has been fanned by politicians and interest groups until there is a widespread *misperception* that pharmaceutical costs are the primary reason that healthcare is more expensive in the United States than elsewhere. Yet, prescription drugs only account for ten cents of every US healthcare dollar!

Hence, an initiative to "find out what really works" has a populist, anti-drug company flavor that some politicians find appealing.

Why Is the Federal Government Specifically Involved?

The primary argument for the federal government's direct involvement in CER rests on the economic notion that the information developed by such research is a *public good*—like a new highway, it benefits everyone, regardless of whether or not they invested in its creation! And there is a reasonable case to be made that the public good nature of information has had an impact—in other words, private insurers have been unwilling to invest in CER, despite its potential benefits to them, because it would have equally benefited their "free-loading" competitors. Hence, there's less research than there ought to be to maximize the ability of the healthcare market to produce value. Finally, CMS is the single largest insurer with the most to save—and it doesn't have to fund the effort out of its "profits."

But there are other reasons, as well. First, a great deal of the benefit of CER is downstream—savings may not be realized until some time has passed. A knee replacement that lasts for 50 years may be preferable to one that lasts 10 years on both clinical and cost-effectiveness bases, but if the cost of replacing the knee after 10 years is almost certain to fall to another insurer, there is no incentive to spend more for the longer-lasting knee.

The government, however, generally doesn't lose its patients to other insurers. Once an individual starts on Medicare, they're typically in the "plan" for life. That puts the federal government in a great position to benefit from the downstream impacts of more effective care, whether it provides it or mandates that others provide it.

Finally, let's not forget that the federal government has, in simple dollar terms, a larger interest in efficient healthcare than any other entity. The federal government, including CMS, the Department of Defense, and the Department of Veterans

Affairs, purchases the majority of all healthcare today, and that will grow as the population ages.[3]

The concept of CER is not new. In fact, there have been several federal groups engaged in it for several decades. But the primary source of CER has historically been private industry. Producers of drugs and medical devices are required to present evidence of a product's safety and clinical efficacy to the FDA, and sometimes will also perform head-to-head trials against a top competitor in an attempt to create the basis for a claim of equivalence or superiority. This head-to-head evidence is extremely useful for comparing treatments, but the scope of the evidence—the range of products for which such head-to-head comparisons are available—is limited. In addition, the risk that comparative research will not produce the desired results, and the relatively high cost of producing it regardless of outcome, limit the circumstances under which industry is willing to conduct it.

Individual researchers at academic institutions occasionally conduct CER meta-analyses, and the UK-based Cochrane Collaboration, a nonprofit organization, has used its network of volunteers to conduct systematic reviews of randomized controlled trials since 1993. The *Cochrane Database of Systematic Reviews* currently contains 4,929 complete reviews evaluating the effectiveness of various treatments.

Focus of CER

As we stated earlier, CMS needs to reduce costs immediately and dramatically. Consequently, we anticipate they will focus on the highest-cost drivers of healthcare (see Table 4.1). Interestingly, this list of priority areas is similar to what is seen in other developed countries (e.g., Australia and the United Kingdom).

The CBO has a great deal of influence when it comes to identifying spending priorities. It doesn't make policy (or, strictly speaking, even advocate for specific policies), but its

Table 4.1   Most Expensive Medical Conditions Identified by AHRQ versus Areas of Special Significance to Medicare as Identified by HHS.

Most Expensive Conditions (2008)	Areas of Special Significance to Medicare (2004)
Heart conditions: *$95 billion*	Ischemic heart disease
Trauma disorders: *$74 billion*	N/A
Cancer: *$72 billion*	Cancer
Mental disorders, including depression: *$72 billion*	Dementia, including Alzheimer's disease; depression, and other mood disorders
Osteoarthritis and other joint diseases: *$57 billion*	Arthritis and nontraumatic joint disorders
Asthma and chronic obstructive pulmonary disease: *$54 billion*	Chronic obstructive pulmonary disease
High blood pressure: *$47 billion*	Stroke, including control of hypertension
Type 2 diabetes: *$46 billion*	Diabetes mellitus
Back problems: *$35 billion*	N/A
Normal childbirth: *$35 billion*	N/A
Disorders of the upper GI: *$27 billion*	Peptic ulcer/dyspepsia
Pneumonia: *$14 billion*	Pneumonia

Source: Compiled from data from the Agency for Healthcare Research and Quality (AHRQ) and the US Department of Health and Human Services (HHS).

economists and analysts often help to frame options for consideration, and the numbers provided by the CBO are usually accepted by all sides of a debate in the halls of Congress.

The CBO has written a great deal over the last few years on the topic of comparative effectiveness. It is relatively bullish regarding the potential savings to CMS that a properly structured comparative effectiveness program might allow. Former director, Peter Orszag, has suggested that some $700 billion/ year might be saved throughout the entire healthcare system without adversely impacting health outcomes.

Among the implicit recommendations of the CBO are the following:

- Information about the relative effectiveness of medical products should be matched by incentives for using that information effectively, as those incentives will be required to change practice patterns in ways that will produce substantial savings over the long term. The CBO has also noted that this is likely to require changes to existing legislation.

- Comparative effectiveness studies should incorporate cost effectiveness, as this would allow them to have a bigger impact on CMS's budget than if they only compared clinical effectiveness.

- [E]fforts to bolster comparative effectiveness research should be coordinated by an organization in other words respected and trusted by doctors and other professionals, as this would encourage changes in medical practice.

- Comparative effectiveness research should include all relevant subgroups; failure to do so will result in their not being convincing to healthcare practitioners.

- Research based on meta-analysis and claims data, while less expensive than new head-to-head randomized controlled trials, is less definitive; hence there will be a need for both kinds of research.

- The practical limits to the number of clinical trials that can be conducted at one time require focus on those studies with the potential to save the system a lot of money.

- Electronic health records should be implemented in such a way as to increase the ease and rapidity of outcomes research.

- Deficit spending for comparative effectiveness research is legitimate, as the full cost of such research is likely to outweigh near-term benefits, but in the long term it can be expected to pay for itself many times over.

■ Research should draw heavily upon studies previously conducted by the Cochrane Collaborative and other countries' health services (e.g., the United Kingdom's National Institute for Health and Clinical Excellence [NICE]).

The Institute of Medicine (IOM), a widely respected, non-profit organization chartered to provide authoritative opinions on healthcare issues, also plays a key role in CER and prioritization. The IOM meets the CBO's desired criteria for an organization that would be charged with bolstering comparative effectiveness research and encouraging changes in practice patterns, as it is (a) widely respected by clinicians and others in the healthcare field, and (b) is seen as relatively free of bias.

The IOM has indicated its support for increased funding of comparative effectiveness research, stating that $20 billion/year (a number that it selected because it is 1% of healthcare expenditures) spent on determining what works would clearly improve the ability to get value from healthcare.

The IOM has also cited Kaiser's Archimedes project, a mathematical description of patient health that allows the impact of various interventions to be modeled and assessed with some degree of accuracy, as a way to leverage existing data. They see it as creating an efficient way to develop comparative information on competing therapies. The adoption of such a model would have significant implications for the structure of the health information technology system. Model-suggested research might eventually come to dominate the comparative effectiveness research priorities.

The IOM explicitly advocates evaluation of the costs *and* benefits of therapies *over the lifetime* of the patient, including the possibility of downstream complications and often ignored benefits like increased productivity.

Finally, the Patient Protection and Affordable Care Act (PPACA) defined yet another broad-based independent group to weigh in and oversee research prioritization as well as discuss the implications of such research. The Patient-Centered Outcomes Research Institute (PCORI) was created as an independent organization whose aim is to "help people make informed healthcare decisions and improve healthcare delivery." With appointed representatives from across industry and academia, its primary goal is to commission research, ostensibly informed by public comment periods reflecting the concerns of patients, caregivers, and the broader healthcare community. Its public face emphasizes *patient engagement* and *transparency* in its deliberations. PCORI is staffed and its efforts fully supported by taxpayer dollars. Its existence speaks to the commitment of the Obama administration and Congress to use research and real-world evidence to guide treatments toward those that *work*. Regardless of the organization's relative effectiveness, it is another statement that CER is here to stay and that choices will be made from among available therapies.

Expected Criteria for Choosing Priorities

There are three criteria we believe are likely to make a particular disease state, medical condition, technology, or treatment protocol a target for CER. These include the total current cost to CMS, the projected rate of increase in total cost to CMS, and political hot-button issues.

There are several segments of the healthcare industry that have raised the ire of people in Washington. Some vulnerable products, technologies, or practices within these segments will likely be priorities for CER—not primarily for practical reasons, but for political ones.

These include:

■ High-priced brand drugs used to treat conditions for which cheaper generic competition exists. Similarly, biologics, with their high cost and limited market size, may also be vulnerable if approval of treatments becomes an exercise in logrolling. The introduction of biosimilars will also challenge the biologics market.

■ Products and treatment protocols related to the wound care industry, which has come under Office of Inspector General (OIG) scrutiny over the last few years.

■ Products in the spine and orthopedics industry, in which many of the established manufacturers were subject to deferred prosecution agreements, apparently on suspicion of making false claims and offering kickbacks to surgeons for using or endorsing them. They are still subject to corporate integrity agreements that require extensive federal monitoring and financial penalties.

The implications of CER for specific sectors of the healthcare industry (i.e., delivery; pharmaceutical, medical device, and diagnostics manufacturers; and payers) are discussed in each of the subsequent chapters.

Endnotes

1. *The Impact of Comparative Effectiveness on the Healthcare Marketplace*. Saint Louis: Numerof & Associates, Inc., 2009.
2. Centers for Medicare and Medicaid Services, Office of the Actuary. National Health Statistics Group. *National Healthcare Data Expenditures Data*. January 2012.
3. Centers for Medicare and Medicaid Services, Office of the Actuary, National Health Statistics Group; US Department of Commerce, Bureau of Economic Analysis; and US Bureau of the Census.

Chapter 5

Redesigning Healthcare Delivery: Hospitals Were Never Meant to Be Destinations of Choice

Everyone reading this book knows a painful truth—that hospitals were never meant to be destinations of choice. No matter how beautiful they are—no matter the fountains, marble, and glass—they really aren't resorts.

Hospitals are in the sickness business—not the healthcare business. They get paid to diagnose and treat illness, making more money for doing more things to each patient.

We talk about healthcare as a patient-centered enterprise, but that's not really true either. Anyone who's been a patient in most hospitals knows they are confusing, hard to navigate, and demand an incredible amount of redundant information. Most departments within the hospital have their own information systems and most of those don't speak to each other. Because regulations require the capture of certain information (or maybe because it's needed to ensure the hospital gets paid), basic information is asked over and over again—not between institutions mind you, but between departments within the walls of the hospital. Until recently, the appropriateness of clinical intervention and quality hasn't been linked in any way to payment. And if mistakes were made within the system, hospitals made more money by fixing those mistakes (like medication errors, hospital-acquired infections, falls, inappropriate readmissions, or bounce-backs, etc.). Even now, despite the Centers for Medicare and Medicaid Services' (CMS's) intent to not pay for such *never events*, we're on a path to dilute this nascent connection between payment and outcomes that should have been there from the start.

When financial squeezes have occurred, hospital administrators understandably cut and tightened. However, when you cut corners, run too lean with staff, and deal with sicker and sicker patients in acute care settings, mistakes are much more likely to occur! And we're not suggesting that these errors are made with malicious intent, but the critical focus on accountability for outcomes has been largely absent.

The reality of healthcare is that it's big business. Despite the window dressing, when you get right down to creating change in any industry, it's all about the money—who pays, for what, and how. Economic incentives work in a very nuanced way, consciously and subconsciously, and drive decisions. As long as healthcare delivery continues on the path of fee-for-service reimbursement without regard to outcomes, the tendency to do more/make more will remain strong.

CMS has recognized that changes have to be made, and has instituted some of these in the way it pays for healthcare. Commercial payers are quickly following suit. But current payment is predominantly done on a piecework basis—and when we're trying to change tiny slices of activity, it's really hard to meaningfully redesign the work!

Even as CMS struggles to reduce the cost of care, individual consumers are increasingly burdened by the combination of higher premiums and cost shifting by employers that leave them with a larger percentage of that cost to bear. Inevitably these forces are building consumer pressure for a more market-responsive healthcare delivery system, and all that implies.

Imagine a future where consumers ask questions about the price and outcomes that healthcare systems deliver—not questions about the cost of one MRI versus another, but about *all* the costs to treat a pregnancy or an orthopedic procedure. Today, these areas are relatively easy to calculate as they have a defined beginning, middle, and end. Yet, very few healthcare systems are prepared to answer such questions. Fewer still are able to include the physician, home care, or rehab components. And for those that can offer a price estimate, even fewer are able to provide transparent data on health outcomes or the patient experience compared to competitors.

Without this data, how can a consumer decide to choose one hospital over another when they are just miles apart? This is the future of healthcare, and healthcare systems and independent physicians need to get ready for it.

Adapting to the Changing Landscape of Healthcare

The hospital model today stands in the crosswinds of market and nonmarket forces. On the market side, there is the hard reality that sustainable margin is required for financial viability. On the nonmarket side, there are a host of regulations to comply with, a mission that includes caring for those who can't pay, disproportionate payer bargaining power, and a relative inability to compete on the dimensions of price and quality.

Compounding the problem has been the growing number of freestanding clinics, which are not subject to the same regulations and are able to carve out the most profitable portions of the market for themselves. With newer equipment and lower overhead, they can capture higher margins, and can refer the uninsured and those complex cases that pose the biggest medical and financial risks to the hospital.[1]

Hospitals have been left playing catch-up. To stay competitive, they've needed to upgrade and expand facilities, compete for a shrinking pool of qualified staff, and implement expensive new technology. The ongoing gap between current income and the requirements for continued competitiveness forced the assumption of debt, further increasing overhead.

Looking ahead, the view is even darker. In the aftermath of recession, banks have tightened their requirements for credit, governments are more wary of guarantees they might previously have given, and so capital costs are rising. Worse yet, significant reductions in reimbursement are in process, even as growth in the Medicare population is set to rise to historic levels. Hospitals have previously *cost shifted* to private payers what Medicare didn't pay, but that's sure to meet stiff resistance. Between new regulations and public fury over a decade of premium increases, private payers will not just resist—they will likely follow CMS's lead. This convergence of negative long-term trends won't be adequately addressed by the kinds of cost-cutting tactics that have been typical in the industry for the past few decades. Paired with flat or shrinking margins, this typical situation makes for an unsustainable business model. Something has got to change.

Needed: A Transfusion of Fresh Thinking

For more than a decade, as payers have increasingly squeezed revenues, much of the industry has defined its strategic response as doing what it's always done, but for less. Hospitals aggregated into systems to maximize their leverage with payers and suppliers and "squeeze back" on reimbursement and supplies. Internally, cost-cutting efforts have come and gone, usually with limited long-term impact. The current popularity of Lean and Six Sigma notwithstanding, such efforts have consistently underperformed against expectations. Hobbled by inflated resource requirements, lack of strategic alignment, and implementation that typically fails to make line management accountable, these tactics may capture some savings and process improvement, but offer no guidance toward fixing an outmoded business model.

To get off the "spend and borrow treadmill," hospitals need to redefine the business they are in. For some that means defining themselves, in fact, as a business. While there is no single solution or model that guarantees success, it's clearly time for some out-of-the-box thinking.

One opportunity for thinking differently about healthcare delivery lies in more fully realizing the benefits of scale. Most hospital systems have successfully used their aggregated economic power to negotiate better terms with suppliers and payers, but have hardly begun to leverage all of the competitive advantages that scale offers. Outside of healthcare, multidivisional corporate structures look for synergy across operating units by centralizing support functions, integrating sales forces, and specializing manufacturing. Generally, this hasn't happened in healthcare. Systems need to move more decisively to capture operational improvements by specializing within facilities. This will allow more efficient use of assets as volume increases and efficiency efforts become more focused on core processes, and will help to improve the competitiveness of hospitals with smaller clinics.

The main reason that hospital systems have been slow to capitalize on economies of scale has to do with the culture of healthcare. Most hospitals are local in origin. Whether community based or academic, they have their roots deep in the history of their city or town, and have been shaped by the unique influences and personalities that drove them from their beginnings. When such organizations become part of a larger system, resistance to change is profound. Not infrequently, cultural differences between the acquired and the acquirer are wide enough to cause a rupture in the relationship. More often, such differences are just enough to ensure that the standardization of almost any process means dealing with conflict. Unfortunately, in the culture of healthcare, more so than in most other realms of business, conflict is not dealt with well. The net result is that synergies that could be captured are not.

More radically, hospitals and systems need to more effectively integrate individual practice areas and ancillary treatments into a disease state focus in selective areas. Such integration enables them to capture marketing and expertise synergies, as well as operational efficiencies as fewer core processes are refined and standardized.

Established healthcare delivery organizations also need a more proactive strategy to counter the "cherry picking" of high-margin patients by free-standing clinics. Historically, the most common "strategy" is to enter in to a joint venture reactively, when possible, which simply mitigates the loss. Hospitals need to consider new models of distribution and capital acquisition that will allow them to preempt such competitive activity.

Reconceptualizing delivery models also means considering innovations like walk-in retail diagnostic and testing clinics in supermarkets or convenience stores, staffed by a nurse practitioner with a supervising physician on call for consultation. Entrepreneurial service companies already have broken this ground; forward-thinking corporations have followed suit; hospitals that don't act soon will find themselves shut out.

At its most basic level, this means a shift in thinking from simply cutting costs to actively seeking growth *by doing business differently.* As a first step, hospitals will need to decide what businesses they won't be in, and they'll need to get out of those businesses. It's that first step that improves margins and frees resources for future growth. They also need to think about how to change their cultures to create an environment in which this kind of entrepreneurial activity can flourish. A critical step in this direction is challenging the long-held assumptions (1) that if you practice good medicine, the money will follow; and (2) that clinical and financial activity are independent and should remain separate.

Management Infrastructure

Hospitals have historically found it difficult to implement new strategy. In part that's a result of their diffuse structure. Departments often function as silos, specialization confers power, and resistance to change is high. Too often, line management is not actively engaged by administration in making the case for and supporting change. As a result, change moves slowly or not at all. Paralleling this issue is an even more fundamental one. The management infrastructure in most hospitals is optimized for performing technical tasks, not for meeting strategic business challenges. Managers themselves are usually promoted on the basis of strong technical skills and the ability to execute efficiently within the existing structure, so they are likely to lack the managerial and financial skills that allow them to drive change through the organization, and are often exceptionally resistant to changing the system that worked so well for them.

Effective leaders at all levels of the organization need an understanding of their role that goes beyond technical expertise to encompass things like strategy-directed corporate stewardship and fiscal management. They need to understand where the organization is going and what their role will be in getting there. Without redefining the role of management, and providing the training and tools to support it, most current managers will never reach that point. Most healthcare organizations need to give a lot more attention to this "management infrastructure."

Creating a management infrastructure that supports change is a critical first step for hospitals to remain competitive. This doesn't simply mean putting appropriate Information Technology (IT) in place, or training managers to get information from it (though both are necessary). It means ensuring that managers know what to do with the information once they have it, that they have the skills to use it effectively, and that they understand what their larger purpose within the organization is so that they can use it to further that purpose. If organizations in the industry are to successfully adapt to the changing healthcare landscape, leadership needs to put these challenges at the top of their list.

Misuse of IT

The current administration hails an investment in health information technology (HIT), specifically electronic medical records (EMRs), as one of the keystones of healthcare reform. As Todd Park and Peter Basch noted in their May 2009 article[2] for the Center for American Progress, the effectiveness of this IT utilization will ultimately depend on its alignment with a different payment model.

The healthcare industry has already invested significantly in IT. The irony is that much of the use of IT has been focused on getting paid, not on delivering better outcomes. This represents *another unintended cost consequence* of CMS's implementation of diagnosis-related groups (DRGs) and a lost opportunity to utilize such technology to achieve better outcomes.

As has been well documented, the current payment system pays for the delivery of services performed, not for the quality of healthcare outcomes achieved. It's a payment system that unintentionally punishes providers for achieving efficiencies such as the elimination of avoidable hospital readmissions and unnecessary care. Not surprisingly, hospitals generally haven't pressured the companies that provide health IT solutions for products that support significant improvements in care quality and value. Instead, they've wanted IT solutions to help pick codes for billing purposes and document care for malpractice purposes, not for clinical decision support, care path management, and quality performance reporting.

George Halvorson, CEO of Kaiser Permanente and advocate for change in the healthcare system, also noted the misuse of IT. He has highlighted the irony that such a high-tech, information-dependent profession relies on data captured and stored on inaccessible and illegible scraps of paper. He has also noted the missed opportunities to utilize IT to better disseminate the flow of new medical knowledge, to better coordinate care, and to capture and track outcomes in support of evidence-based medicine.[2]

Virtually every other industry invests in and utilizes technology to compete by providing better products for lower cost. Because of how we pay for healthcare, however, the industry has historically used IT poorly. It has underinvested in IT because there's been no incentive to improve efficiency or outcomes, leaving the government to mandate and finance the investment. And its primary use of IT has been to manage the administrative nightmare of getting paid, with little discernible impact on improved outcomes or lower cost—the objectives we have now set for healthcare reform.

This critical IT investment program now underway will fail if it embraces technology adoption for the sake of adoption alone. But if this new IT investment is wedded to a strong commitment to provider payment reform and implemented as an accelerator of healthcare delivery innovation, then the investment can help transform US healthcare as we know it.

Comparative Effectiveness Research Is Shaping Healthcare Delivery

As time goes on, the healthcare delivery marketplace will be heavily impacted by comparative effectiveness research (CER).[3] Most fundamentally, those in the industry need to realize that this research is primarily a means to the end of reducing

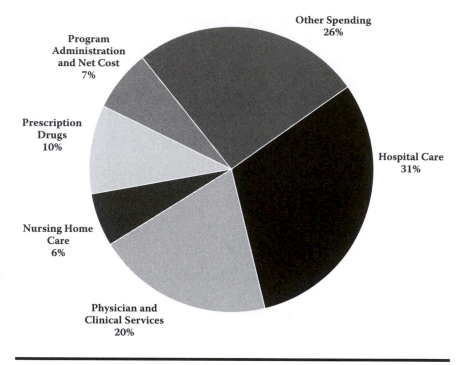

Figure 5.1   Where the nation's health dollar went in calendar year 2010. Other Spending includes dental and other professional services, home health, durable medical products, over-the-counter medicines and sundries, public health, other personal healthcare, research, and structures and equipment. (Compiled from Centers for Medicare and Medicaid Services, Office of the Actuary, National Health Statistics Group, *National Healthcare Expenditures Data, January 2012.*)

CMS's healthcare expenditures. Given that payments to the providers of healthcare (hospitals, physicians, and nursing homes) account for the lion's share of total expenditures (see Figure 5.1), those same providers are likely to see the largest reduction in revenues.

The two most important impacts of CER for the healthcare delivery industry are expected to be the development of predictive care paths and a significant change in quality metrics. Each of these is discussed below.

Development of Predictive Care Paths

As we described in Chapter 4, CER is not restricted to research into what products work best—it also includes research into what *treatment protocols* work best. Existing protocols will come under scrutiny, under the same general terms as other products, and ultimately, are likely to be subject to mandatory guidelines. While deviation may not be "illegal," it may not be reimbursed.

The implication for hospitals is really clear: take control and define your outcomes or someone else will do it for you.

These guidelines are expected to impact the projected *priority areas* earliest and most strongly. And, at the time of this writing, the priorities are continuously evolving. Providers deriving a large portion of revenues or profits through cardiovascular centers, orthopedics, or bariatric surgery are likely to face the largest, most immediate risks.

Changing Quality Metrics

Traditional quality metrics such as those used by Healthgrades (measures of mortality and morbidity) are in the process of being replaced by a combination of process metrics (measuring compliance with "recommended" treatment guidelines) and outcome metrics that integrate patient quality of life into mortality and morbidity metrics. This will take place as part of the shift from a focus on gross *clinical* effectiveness to a focus on *cost* effectiveness, because cost effectiveness is nearly universally defined to include quality of life (e.g., the QALY, or quality-adjusted life year).

Impact of CER on Hospital Operations

We expect that fiscal austerity and CER will have two main effects on hospitals. The first is the reduction in revenues that comes from fewer, and less expensive, procedures being performed. This is a direct consequence of CMS's need to save money, starting with lower and more restrictive reimbursement, followed by guidelines and treatment protocols. The point of the treatment protocols will be enhanced cost effectiveness, even though the protocols may result in some improvements on the clinical effectiveness side.

The baseline expectation is that attempts will be made to continue to push care down the acuity hierarchy, with the goal of preventing the most expensive procedures. The likely result will be more reliance on objective tests to identify patients who are expected to have a good response to less expensive procedures and therapies—drugs instead of surgery, lifestyle changes instead of drugs, outpatient treatment instead of inpatient, and home care instead of care within a medical facility. Those hospitals that have invested heavily in plant and capital equipment to deliver the most advanced care in service line areas like cardiovascular disease and orthopedics may find their return on these investments significantly reduced relative to their expectations.

The second effect is, at least potentially, the reduced ability to differentiate based on care protocols that are not evidence based. Currently, this is a growing element of the branding efforts of hospitals and hospital systems. In the future, differentiation will come from more effective execution of "standard" protocols, as reflected in new outcome metrics and the presentation of specific economic and clinical value data.

To the extent that new protocols are developed, they'll be subject to much more stringent requirements regarding payment, and it's likely that they'll be developed in partnership with pharmaceutical, medical device, or diagnostics manufacturers who will partially fund the generation of cost-effectiveness evidence for protocols incorporating their products. As an example, a device maker might develop equipment for monitoring the weight of patients with congestive heart failure (in whom rapid weight gain may be a sign of impending trouble) and automatically transmitting that information back to a physician. This has the potential to save a trip to the acute care setting. Should the protocol be adopted as the standard of care, the provider and device manufacturer will both benefit. We anticipate the use of these guidelines to pick up immediately. Changes to legislation to allow enforcement through the reimbursement system are likely to follow shortly.

For an industry that currently struggles to avoid never events like leaving surgical instruments inside a patient, the change to process metrics will be especially difficult. Compliance with prescribed care paths will require a new managerial infrastructure that aligns the roles, accountabilities, and incentives of all members of the organization, including physicians, to ensure adequate focus on compliance, without losing sight of their strategic accountabilities.

In 2009, in *The Impact of Comparative Effectiveness on the Healthcare Marketplace: A Special Report*, we projected the timing for these changes to be three years. So far this projection has proved to be accurate. Changes to quality metrics have been integrated into CMS's larger healthcare reform package in its accountable care organization (ACO) experiments beginning in 2012, with similar initiatives in various stages of development on the commercial side. CER will inform the selection of quality metrics, but for the most part they will reflect a top-down decision based on already existing knowledge. Guidance regarding the new quality metrics was issued by the US Department of Health and Human Services (HHS) as part of the Health Information Technology initiative early in 2012.

Prudent Responses and Defensive Strategies

At this point, we continue to recommend that healthcare delivery organizations pursue four key strategic and defensive responses:

- Insulate against the impact of the shrinking pie.
- Position to benefit from cost savings.
- Anticipate changes to the reimbursement scheme.

■ Optimize treatment protocols today.

We discuss each of these below.

Insulate from the impact of the shrinking pie: The most obvious, and probably most prudent, way to create this insulation is to begin to diversify sources of revenue away from insurers (including, but not limited to, CMS) and toward direct payment for service. Examples include the development of walk-in retail clinics (some of which may not take health insurance and offer services for about the cost of a typical copay), the creation of premium services or accommodations within the hospital, and a shift toward providing elective medical services.

The movement will be to shift the locus of care out of the acute care setting to ambulatory care in local clinics, other distributed settings, and ultimately, the home. Increasing the convenience of care tends to put more control over health decisions in the hands of patients, which increases the likelihood that their unique needs—for the reassurance that diagnostic testing or a clinical opinion provides, or for an elective procedure—will be met regardless of the calculated cost effectiveness of these interventions for the population as a whole.

It might even be possible to develop a business model centered around educated consumers who place a greater premium on quality of care than Medicare is likely to provide and are willing to pay out of pocket (either instead of or in addition to standard reimbursement) to obtain it.

Position to benefit from cost savings: If a provider can determine how CMS will ultimately structure work to save cost, it may be able to benefit by allying with manufacturers in the development of treatment approaches (incorporating effective and efficient treatment protocols and new or modified products that make those protocols effective) that will be adopted by CMS as the "gold standard" for treatment. Manufacturers are already beginning to see their products come under pressure from an economic value perspective. They would welcome a partner with ideas for using these products, even if in modified form, in ways that maximize their value, and hence the likelihood of continued reimbursement.

The other way providers can position themselves to capitalize from cost savings is to preemptively implement the organizational changes that will allow them to outcompete their competition after the changes come. These changes include a more sophisticated, integrated, and effective managerial infrastructure, as well as the implementation of information technology that correctly anticipates the demands of the Health Information Technology initiative.

Government is not (yet) mandating framework and structure for this information technology—just saying that it must be in place. While the government has defined expectations for *meaningful use*, there are no defined incentives to ensure that integration takes place. But there is an opportunity for forward-looking healthcare delivery systems to lead the design of this architecture and create an integrated approach.

Don't underestimate the difficulty of this work, however, or the criticality of getting it right. And be wary of the idea that the right information technology infrastructure will, by itself, break down silos that exist within and across sites of care. Change is necessary to improve outcomes and reduce the cost of care, but it can only come about when the right human infrastructure is in place, ensuring alignment with strategic goals, coordination across roles, and appropriate accountabilities and incentives. The cultural shifts that must occur within the organization are enormous.

Anticipate changes to the reimbursement scheme: To the extent that providers can anticipate what disease states will be most heavily and quickly impacted, and are able to diversify away from those areas (or avoid additional investment in them), they will reduce the risks associated with these areas. Even today, delaying the purchase of capital equipment associated with the projected priority areas (and acute care areas more broadly) is prudent. Reevaluation of the risks and likely return on such equipment is needed.

It is clear, however, that the service line centers of excellence that many hospitals have made a strategic priority show an uncanny level of overlap with the priority areas for cost reduction identified previously. Cardiovascular disease, cancer, diabetes, and osteoarthritis are all likely to be subject to intense pressure through the reimbursement system over the next several years.

This will tend to reduce the return on investment for these areas, and the challenge will be to replace the lost revenue by broadening the focus within the targeted disease states. This may mean that the capital, equipment, and personnel brought on board in the expectation of a large influx in acute care will instead be redeployed from the acute setting to ambulatory and lifestyle interventions, and possibly long-term care.

The other major change in other words likely to happen is the creation of incentives for maintaining wellness outside the hospital setting. Reimbursement for wellness programs will be based on studies conducted through CER, and the incorporation of *prevention* into healthcare standards will be held up as a major coup for the initiative.

Optimize treatment protocols today: The need to control costs that's behind CER funding means that DRG reimbursement levels will become increasingly stingy, even while quality metrics become increasingly broad. In response, providers will have to perform their own form of CER. This will mean evaluating new technologies in the context of care within the hospital, adding them only if they improve outcomes, decrease cost, or both, and eliminating those that no longer add to the cost effectiveness of care. All acquisitions of capital equipment, and even the addition of tests to be run on existing equipment, will be evaluated in the context of economic and clinical value. The challenge will be to identify and develop standardized practices supported by a base of evidence drawn from within the institution incorporating medical society guidelines as appropriate.

The use of an optimized set of diagnostic tests to guide physicians in choosing the most cost-effective course of treatment for patients is an area in other words especially ripe for improvement. Hospitals have already started to demand that manufacturers provide evidence of the economic and clinical value of diagnostic tests, how they should be used, how much they will cost, what costs can be eliminated, and what the benefits will be. The extent of these demands for evidence will, and should, increase.

Accountable Care Is Needed, ACOs Are Not

The Patient Protection and Affordable Care Act (PPACA) of 2010 created a new, federally financed mechanism for healthcare delivery via Medicare: the accountable care organization (ACO). As we write this, the constitutionality of the legislation is currently under review by the US Supreme Court. Regardless of the outcome, the ACO concept has been raised to prominence by its promotion in the legislation as an answer to the problems with the US healthcare system. Proponents of the concept will likely press forward for ACO implementation in any case. Our position, based on decades of direct experience working with healthcare stakeholders, is that such action would be a mistake.

As we noted in the ACO policy paper we wrote for The Heritage Foundation,[4] ACOs are merely the latest in a long history of health policy "silver bullets." Since the 1970s, Congress and successive administrations have promoted a number of mechanisms to control rising healthcare costs, including the introduction of Medicare hospital payment formulas based on fixed payments for hospital services (payments for DRGs), health maintenance organizations (HMOs), and preferred provider organizations (PPOs). Yet costs have continued to rise despite these efforts. At the same time, concerns about fragmentation of care and diminished quality have increased significantly.

ACOs have been promoted as a new mechanism for addressing the shortcomings of previous reforms.[5] Congress, apparently unmindful of legislating an untested model in a field as complex as healthcare, included provisions in the PPACA to establish accountable care organizations.[6] Only loosely defined by the original legislation, ACOs consist of groups of physicians and other providers that work together to manage and coordinate care for Medicare fee-for-service beneficiaries, and to meet certain quality-performance standards. Through shared savings programs, ACOs will receive a portion of the shared savings if they sufficiently reduce costs and simultaneously improve quality.

Curiously, under the statute, the secretary of HHS is charged with developing a method to assign Medicare beneficiaries to ACOs.[7] Because the statute is unclear about the resolution of many vital issues, the crucial details will be supplied and refined by federal regulators—as is the case for so many other provisions of the new health law—if it survives judicial review. When the initial set of rules came out in April 2011, the more than 500 pages of Byzantine guidance were met by so much negativity by "model" ACOs that CMS backed off and modified its requirements. At the time of this writing the rules are still in formation, the initial flaws we saw in the original legislation persist, and we expect these experiments to waste taxpayer dollars. Rather than improving health outcomes and lowering cost, we expect ACOs as envisioned by CMS to make things worse.

Laudable Goals

The stated goal of an ACO is laudable—to reduce costs and improve quality of care through cooperation and coordination among providers. While a number of potential models were proposed before the PPACA was passed, the legislation incorporated a model that doesn't exist in practice. Each of the proposed models, including the one incorporated in PPACA, has a unique set of drawbacks, limitations, and difficulties. Creating a new organizational structure to remedy problems inherent in the existing system creates complications and risks. These complications are likely to result in the same or similar types of unintended consequences as earlier efforts, namely, consolidation and increased costs without improvements in quality.

It is unlikely that an untested organizational structure will be the most effective way to create accountability for care. In theory, the ACO program "promotes accountability for a patient population and coordinates items and services ... and encourages investment in infrastructure and redesigned care processes for high quality and efficient service delivery."[8] However, the likely result will be a concentration of power not in the most efficient and highest-quality healthcare organizations, but in the largest—simply because they control large segments of the market share. Since the law was passed, we've seen dramatic consolidation across the country as physicians—primary care and even specialties once fiercely independent such as cardiovascular and orthopedic surgeons join the "safe haven" of employment by hospitals.

Any Provider Can Provide More Accountable Care

Nothing is (or ever has been) keeping any provider from creating more accountable care. Whether or not an ACO structure is an effective means to achieve this end is irrelevant. Rather than focusing on restructuring, organizations should really be thinking about how to ensure that there is basic accountability across the system.

Let's take the example of aseptic technique and the basic act of handwashing, a perennial compliance problem for many healthcare delivery organizations across the country. In a nutshell, hospitals have been challenged to enforce the expectation that healthcare providers, including physicians, wash their hands between patient encounters. Failure to comply with the practice is associated with the spread of hospital-acquired infections (HAIs) and astronomical costs—tens of thousands of deaths per year. The lack of public outrage regarding this is pretty remarkable.

Let's put this in proper perspective. In the 2010 Toyota brake recall, 37 people allegedly due to negligence, lost their lives, and the congressional debate was deafening. There hasn't been a corresponding outcry regarding healthcare safety issues despite the numbers. Ironically, PPACA provides for financial incentives to help hospitals reduce medication errors, HAIs, and so on. In industries subject to market forces, such tolerance wouldn't occur.

In high-tech, for instance, stringent procedures are expected and followed in making microchips. Everyone understands the costs to the business if the sterile field isn't maintained in designated clean rooms. In healthcare it hasn't worked the same way. Administrators express fatigue at trying to get physicians and other staff to comply with the basic rules, often putting responsibility for policy adherence on patients and visitors! This is clearly a failure of accountability—a failure of leadership to articulate a clear set of expectations and then consistently enforce a basic set of rules with consequences for nonadherence.

So, beyond basic individual accountability for legitimate procedural compliance, with or without an ACO, here's what it takes to provide accountable care more broadly:

1. **Establish key process metrics (e.g., costs by procedure, patient cycle time to key behavioral milestones):** Use this data in real time to manage cost variability and to identify opportunities to improve efficiency.
2. **Establish meaningful quality and outcome metrics:** Use this data to manage variability as well as to improve quality and outcomes. Make performance matter.

3. **Develop predictive care paths that reflect evidence-based medicine:** Mapping out your process for delivering care is essential to ensuring collaboration and accountability, managing variability, and improving clinical practice across your organization. But it can't look like the efforts of yesteryear with minute provider prescriptive activity. Effective predictive care paths that reflect the continuum of care (versus narrow episodes) are patient centered and reflect clinical decision making, thus allowing patients to better understand what's likely to happen *and* enabling physicians to do what's required for a specific patient. While achieving behavioral change can be difficult, incorporating evidence-based practice will support the objective of achieving better outcomes at lower cost. Additionally, external research can serve as a benchmark for your organization's improvement efforts.

4. **Develop competencies and incentives that drive increased accountability:** Engage in process redesign that really redesigns care across the continuum and change management that enables clinicians to be more effective in monitoring, evaluating, and improving outcomes while controlling costs. Establish performance expectations and incentive structures to ensure greater ownership.

5. **Take steps to facilitate provider coordination:** Your organization should be a vehicle for effective, efficient, and transparent provider collaboration. Developing the IT and system integration capabilities to implement a uniform Electronic Health Records (EHR) system that will allow providers to communicate with each other more seamlessly is key. However, it has to include tools that enable real-time feedback, reflect clinical decision making, and facilitate trend analysis across the continuum of care on a patient-specific and group basis.

These steps are not easy to operationalize. They require an integrated effort and shared accountability between administrative and clinical leaders. They also require organizations to set cost and quality goals that go hand in hand—they cannot be segregated and addressed independently. All decisions in the care model have to be in the dual context of the economic *and* clinical value that would result. Accountable care is about improving this dual value proposition.

What Are You Waiting For?

As we've suggested, there isn't anything holding health systems back. There is, though, a rare market opportunity to seize the initiative and deliver more accountable care. Improving accountability will differentiate organizations in an increasingly competitive market in which cost and quality outcomes are growing more critical to success.

How well each of these interventions works depends in part on the development of a new underlying payment mechanism in other words transparent, predictive, and inclusive— bundled pricing. We explore that next.

Bundled Payment: The Next Step in Improving Quality and Reducing Cost

Although the main focus of reform legislation has been on improving access through regulation of healthcare insurance, its implications for the healthcare delivery industry are profound and will require truly innovative change. We have discussed throughout the book that fee-for-service payment is now being openly challenged—not because fee-for-service is problematic in and of itself, but because it has been *unconnected to outcomes and has driven up utilization.* PPACA authorized ongoing experimentation on alternative payment mechanisms that could profoundly alter market dynamics for healthcare delivery. Commercial insurers are in pursuit of similar objectives. Whatever the fate of PPACA, this issue will not go away. Delivery organizations must choose to dramatically challenge key assumptions about the care they deliver or risk their financial viability.

As we argued at the start of this chapter, most hospitals have learned to manage financially with the discounted fee-for-service model that's been in place, but that's history. At this point, hospitals face a payer mix in which government's share is increasing, while its reimbursement rate continues to shrink. To make matters worse, private payers—no longer free to ride the cost curve up—will be following government's lead more than ever. With nowhere to turn to recover its losses on government reimbursement, the sector needs to develop new ways to manage costs and to make good on demands for increased quality. And it needs to be prepared to assume risk for the care it delivers in an increasingly transparent manner.

The answer is *value-based payment*, or specifically, *bundled payment*.[9] Traditional approaches to cost management are clearly not up to the job, and anyway, providers may not *have* a choice—bundled payment may become a competitive requirement, and for most institutions, the decision to provide services in this way requires a paradigm change.

Why Will Bundled Payment Models Do Any Better?

Promising to deliver a standardized set of services for a fixed price with specific quality guarantees will finally force care providers to align their efforts to contain underlying cost drivers. Taking action on such issues as overutilization, technology choices, and inadequate coordination across the care continuum can drive meaningful change in cost and quality, but only if providers are uniformly focused on these outcomes, without the distortions caused by the current fee-for-service approach. A concurrent focus on development of a differentiated clinical value case will ensure a balanced approach that doesn't forgo quality and safety for the sake of economic efficiency. Such efforts require major paradigm shifts in thinking at the top and new competencies and focus within the management infrastructure.

So How Do We Get There?

Healthcare executives who want to prepare for bundled pricing models will need to take these five steps:

1. *Examine their current economic and clinical value proposition:* Healthcare delivery organizations will need to identify their own strengths and gaps. This will help identify where to start, what services are already delivering good outcomes, and where practices can be improved.
2. *Identify cost drivers in key services:* Clinical, technical, and process elements all factor into the total cost of healthcare. Providers will need to create the infrastructure to address inefficiencies and distinguish *necessary* from *unnecessary* variability.
3. *Develop predictive care paths:* Predictive care paths should capture key decision points that have an impact on costs and outcomes, and include differentiators that set the delivery organization apart. They should be *patient centric*—better yet, consumer centric—mapping care from the consumer's perspective across the episode. These will need to be implemented across the continuum of care to help track variability in cost and quality.
4. *Collaborate with payers:* In order to move reimbursement away from episodic care, providers implementing bundled pricing will need to collaborate with payers. By examining the economic and clinical value of the services included in the bundle, and systematically capturing key

differentiators, providers will be able to make a strong value case for the care they deliver.

5. *Continuously monitor and update bundled services:* This includes both internal monitoring for compliance and external review, to ensure that their organizations stay current with ongoing research. This will help guarantee that treatment protocols continue to deliver better care at lower cost.

Healthcare executives *must* prepare now for new payment models, because adapting will not be easy or quick. They will have to implement integrated, systemic changes to remain viable. Times of transition can be extremely challenging, but also extraordinarily rewarding for those who seize the opportunities.

St. Elsewhere: A Case Study in Bundled Pricing

To illustrate the steps for creating a bundled price, let's examine the experience of a specialty, national hospital we'll call *St. Elsewhere*.

St. Elsewhere competes by attracting patients across the United States who have a local, community care provider option. From its inception, St. Elsewhere offered something different—a more integrated and comprehensive care approach that it believed improved patient outcomes and that patients experienced as centered on them.

To succeed in this effort and capture market share, the hospital needed to create a compelling argument for both the *cost and value* of its unique approach. This required:

Establishing predictive care paths: St. Elsewhere needed to ensure that treatment protocols reflecting the practice of its unique course of treatment would be followed in a consistent fashion. Reducing practice variability and understanding the causes of it are essential to any attempt at bundled payment.

Creating an economic and clinical value model:
St. Elsewhere also needed to define the key economic and
clinical components of value to patients and payers that were
realized with its unique care approach. This model guided the
development of the evidence needed to demonstrate better
health outcomes and commensurate value for their price. More
importantly, the model served as a basis for setting a higher
bar in the industry, redefining the quality metrics that would
be used as a comparator between institutions.

Creating a resource utilization model: St. Elsewhere needed
to identify the key drivers of treatment cost and variability.
This required an understanding of the organizational infrastructure (e.g., data and people resources, management tools
for understanding variability, mechanisms for managing variability) necessary to implement fiscally safe new pricing. The
resulting model enabled setting a transparent, fixed price
for the total course of treatment. Setting this price required
certainty that it would cover predictable costs and provide
an adequate margin, without building in a safety factor that
would make the bundled price cost prohibitive.

Taking a Proactive Approach to a Market in Transition

In a market demanding better outcomes at lower cost, St.
Elsewhere is now poised to respond to this demand and to
accelerate growth at healthy margins. As healthcare costs
have spiraled out of control and the daily headlines shout out
the latest quality snafus, it was inevitable that demand for
better care at lower cost would escalate. St. Elsewhere anticipated and prepared to meet this inevitable demand, investing in the models and infrastructure to develop a better care
approach and to prove it. As a result, where other hospitals
see a gathering storm of reduced reimbursements and shrinking margins, St. Elsewhere sees an opportunity to grow share
and preserve margin.

Competing with a Bundled Price

Defining a care path and corresponding price doesn't necessarily result in growth or improved margins.[10] The care that's offered has to be differentiated, delivering more value as defined by the healthcare consumer.

The market share winners in this environment will be those providers who can define and deliver on better health outcome metrics, and these need to go beyond traditional mortality and morbidity measures. Managing health to avoid expensive inpatient care is one of the most obvious consumer objectives.

Competing with a bundled price also requires considerable transparency of information responsive to the needs of a more engaged, value-conscious consumer. The customer of the future wants comparable evidence of health outcomes delivered for a set total price. As in any other market, the winning supplier will have the best answer to the question, "What am I getting for my money?"

Endnotes

1. "Adapting to the Changing Landscape of Healthcare," by Michael N. Abrams and Mark Morgan, *H&HN Online,* April 2007.
2. Todd Park and Peter Basch. *A Historic Opportunity: Wedding Health Information Technology to Care Delivery Innovation and Provider Payment Reform*, Center for American Progress, May 2009.
3. George Halvorson, *Health Care Reform Now! A Prescription for Change* (San Francisco: Jossey-Bass, 2007).
4. *The Impact of Comparative Effectiveness on the Healthcare Marketplace* (St. Louis: Numerof & Associates, Inc., 2009).
5. *Why Accountable Care Organizations Won't Deliver Better Health Care—and Market Innovation Will*, Heritage Foundation, April 18, 2011, http://www.heritage.org/research/reports/2011/04/why-accountable-care-organizations-wont-deliver-better-health-care-and-market-innovation-will.

6. Elliott S. Fisher, Douglas O. Staiger, Julie P. W. Bynum, and Daniel J. Gottlieb, "Creating Accountable Care Organizations: The Extended Hospital Medical Staff," *Health Affairs* 26, no. 1 (2007), w44–w46; http://content.healthaffairs.org/cgi/reprint/26/1/w44 (accessed March 30, 2011).
7. Patient Protection and Affordable Care Act of 2009, H.R. 3690, 111th Cong. (2009), Sec. 3022, "Medicare Shared Savings Program."
8. Grace-Marie Turner et al., *Why Obamacare Is Wrong for America* (New York: Harper Collins, 2011), 63. The US Department of Health and Human Services issued proposed rules for ACOs in the press release, "Affordable Care Act to Improve Quality of Care for People with Medicare," March 31, 2011, http://www.hhs.gov/news/press/2011pres/03/20110331a.html.
9. Patient Protection and Affordable Care Act, Sec. 3022. "Medicare Shared Savings Program."
10. "Bundled Pricing: Strategies for Success" by Eric Abrams, *Becker's Hospital Review*, November 7, 2011.
11. "The Case for Bundled Payments" by Rita E. Numerof and Bill Ott, *H&HN Online*, July 19, 2010.

Chapter 6

A Brave New World for Payers

As we've been arguing, the United States has reached the point where key constituent groups have significant economic and financial concerns—providers and physicians about their revenues, and payers and patients about the affordability of care. At the heart of any discussion about healthcare reform is an increasingly clear mandate to provide *better care at lower cost*. Health policy shifts are placing increased accountability and cost pressures on providers to improve patient safety, quality of care, and consistency of care delivered, and payers and consumers alike are increasing their demands for improved economic and clinical value (ECV).

After years of steadily building pressure from escalating patient care and subsequent healthcare insurance premium costs, the US healthcare system has reached a tipping point. With the passage of the Patient Protection and Affordable Care Act (PPACA) and the Healthcare and Education Reconciliation Act of 2010 (HCERA), the country has irrevocably acknowledged that change must occur, and quickly, to head off financial insolvency. While the legislation left no healthcare stakeholder untouched, the most profound interventions were reserved for insurers.

Let's face it—insurers are the one segment of the healthcare industry that everyone has loved to hate. Insurers are being squeezed on all sides. Employers blame insurers for the rising costs of healthcare; physicians and hospitals blame insurers for their declining reimbursement rates; consumers blame insurers for lack of sufficient coverage and many decry inadequate services as well as opaque rules and payment terms; and policymakers think insurers make too much money.

The legislation was intended to disrupt this status quo, and it has done so. It forces insurance companies to reassess their business models, identify new market opportunities, and take action or suffer financial consequences. New regulatory requirements impose constraints on investment, and by standardizing benefit profiles, accelerate commoditization of products. By the same token, the legislation creates opportunities, especially for those who can recognize them and translate their implications into action in a timely way.

Adapting to the Changing Landscape of Healthcare Insurance

Clearly, the healthcare insurance business model today stands in the crosswinds of market and nonmarket forces.[1] On the market side, there is now a daunting challenge to remain competitive in order to sustain, much less increase, market share and margin. The constantly escalating costs of healthcare, increasingly passed on to consumers by their employers and health insurers, have pushed consumers to the brink (see Figure 6.1). Employers are seeking ways to reduce costs by reducing coverage options, thereby limiting the choices their employees have for insurance.

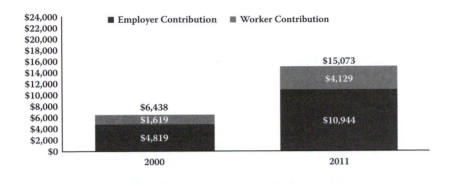

Figure 6.1 Workers's contribution to health insurance premiums rose by $2,510, more than doubling since 2000. (From *Employer Health Benefits, 2010 Summary of Findings*, Kaiser Family Foundation, September 2011.)

On the nonmarket side, the Obama administration has taken on the cause of those who have seemingly fallen through the cracks of America's private healthcare insurance system. From a beachhead of Medicare and Medicaid, some in our government continue to threaten to become a new competitor for the insurance needs of *all* Americans, and without the constraint of having to remain financially viable at the end of the day.

As we laid out in Chapter 2, as the national debate over healthcare reform rages on, there are some fundamental things about which most people agree—the need to achieve better care outcomes at lower cost, and the need to change what gets paid for and how. Increasing demand for value, flat or shrinking market shares and margins, and the looming cloud of government intervention all make for an unsustainable private insurance business model. Clearly, something has to change.

The operating environment for insurers is characterized by conflicting pressures and new demands, as depicted in Figure 6.2. Insurers face conflicting demands from customers (employers and members) and network providers: networks and employers want insurers to help deliver higher-quality health outcomes at lower cost, but also want insurers to maintain the broadest possible providers want higher

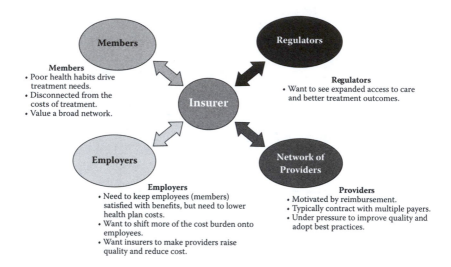

Members
- Poor health habits drive treatment needs.
- Disconnected from the costs of treatment.
- Value a broad network.

Regulators
- Want to see expanded access to care and better treatment outcomes.

Employers
- Need to keep employees (members) satisfied with benefits, but need to lower health plan costs.
- Want to shift more of the cost burden onto employees.
- Want insurers to make providers raise quality and reduce cost.

Providers
- Motivated by reimbursement.
- Typically contract with multiple payers.
- Under pressure to improve quality and adopt best practices.

Figure 6.2   The conflicting pressures for insurers.

reimbursement for medical treatments, but employers and members want lower; networks. These conflicting demands can result in reduced leverage for insurers, in other words, pushing providers too hard to make improvements in cost and quality may result in their leaving the network, reducing its attractiveness.

The disconnect between the decision makers (patients and providers) and the source for payment (insurers and employers) is forcing insurers to intervene as never before to slow the trend of rising treatment costs. New mandates, such as medical loss ratios (MLRs), the Essential Healthcare Benefits (EHB) package, insurance exchanges, and accountable care organizations (ACOs) further complicate the ability of insurers to respond to these conflicting pressures, introducing additional risk and uncertainty. Nontraditional organizations like hospitals and IT companies are moving into the space long held by commercial insurers. Some major IT providers and others are developing models to "manage" the cost of healthcare, support self-insured programs, and develop third-party administrator (TPA) capability. Conversely, insurers are purchasing healthcare delivery organizations, blurring traditional lines of business.

This opens up an opportunity for insurers who want to differentiate themselves competitively to build network loyalty, and superior margins if they can develop their capability to collaborate with providers in developing new care delivery approaches. This requires that payers think outside the box about the products/services provided, build more effective communication mechanisms with providers, and leverage technology and data assets responsively to deliver outcomes of mutual interest.

Needed Here, Too: A Transfusion of Fresh Thinking

As the financial dynamics of the market have become increasingly challenging, much of the healthcare insurance industry has defined its strategic response as doing what it's always done, but for less. Insurers have gotten tougher in negotiations with providers and employers in order to pay for less. And repeated internal cost-cutting efforts have come and gone, usually with limited long-term impact and often contributing to an increasingly cynical and jaded workforce (with a predictable negative effect on customer service).

To get off this cost-cutting spiral—which isn't much help in winning and keeping customers—healthcare insurers need to redefine the business they are in. While there is no single solution or model that guarantees success, it's clearly time for some out-of-the-box thinking.

Rethinking *the Customer*

Most people get their healthcare insurance from their employer. This model started when employers could attract and retain employees with a benefit of fully paid health insurance, which at the time cost less than competing for employees based on compensation alone. This model worked well for insurers, who could focus on the employer as *the customer* and differentiate their insurance offerings based on service rather than price. The model also worked well for employers, who could tie employees into attractive benefit packages. What this model never did was focus on or satisfy the varied needs of the healthcare consumer/employee.

Now employers would love to get out of the business. Every calendar year is another exercise in explaining to financially stressed employees why they have to pay a larger share of more expensive insurance. And when these employers meet with insurance companies the focus of negotiations is on price, not value-added service. The result is that health insurance has suddenly become mostly a commoditized business, where sustaining, much less improving margins is increasingly difficult.

Companies in other consumer product industries have become very innovative in selling to their "real" customers directly, eliminating traditional pseudo customer distribution channels when they no longer add value. If employers were to exit as mediators of individual coverage, payers could wind up understanding their customer needs better, tailoring products to those needs, and capturing a high share of distinct subsets of customers who will pay for their brand and stay loyal to it. Rethinking *the customer* would be an equally suitable place to start for healthcare insurers as they define a more viable business model.

Employers and consumers are reacting to the rising costs of health plans that have followed or exceeded medical cost inflation. Employees, and other consumers of healthcare, have to shoulder a larger portion of the costs of their care in the form of higher premiums, higher copays, high-deductible health plans, and health savings accounts, and this is driving a consumer orientation trend in the market. Patients, as consumers, increasingly want to purchase healthcare services much

like they make other purchasing decisions, by evaluating cost
and quality in pursuit of value.

Rethinking *Products*

Earlier in this book we discussed two significant elements that
have converged to fuel the drive for healthcare reform. One
element is the yearly, sometimes double-digit increase in premium costs. The other element is the macro statistical picture
indicating that Americans (or their employers or government)
pay more for healthcare than in other countries, but aren't
necessarily receiving better care by any outcome measure
currently in use. A key underlying assumption derived from
these statistics is that a significant amount of healthcare services being provided—and paid for—is either unnecessary or
ineffective. As we noted in Chapter 2, many industry leaders
estimate that 30–40% of costs are due to services not needed,
upcoding, medical errors, and process issues.

As consumers continue to feel firsthand the increasing burden of their healthcare costs, they are beginning to act more
and more like customers, demanding value for their money
and proof of that value. Providers and insurers have to engi-
neer the right products to remain competitive in this market.
Leading companies are starting to collaborate to develop and
implement plans for evidence-based medicine and disease
management programs that are less costly and more effective
over a consumer's lifetime.

One of the most critical success factors for such programs
will be the proper alignment of payment with results, providing incentives for the right provider *and* consumer behaviors
in order to achieve measurably better health outcomes.

These new types of products will also challenge healthcare
insurers to change how they measure success. There is general
agreement that integrated care over a continuum will result
in better outcomes at lower cost. This isn't possible without

long-term customer retention and metrics based on total cost versus episodic costs. Insurers will need to learn how to measure and quantify the lifetime value of a customer and make decisions accordingly.

Implications for Healthcare Insurers

Leading insurers must commit to "bending the trend," in other words, slowing the growth in treatment costs, working to reduce healthcare expenditures, and improving health and care outcomes *across the continuum of care.* In a nutshell, it's about creating value. Insurers can directly slow the growth in treatment costs by denying reimbursement for clearly unnecessary care such as medical errors, adverse events, or fraud and waste. The Centers for Medicare and Medicaid Services (CMS) has paved the way to make this normatively acceptable by introducing never events. Since insurers typically lack direct leverage, they have to find new ways to influence behaviors and choices on the part of employers, their members, and providers.

Payers have the power to influence the behavior of policy holders and network providers. They can influence, but not control, the choices made by employers and members by offering lower-cost alternatives, highlighting star performers in their network, and rewarding members for accepting accountability for their health. They can also influence providers to adopt higher-quality care processes and other methods that result in lower treatment costs and better outcomes across the continuum of care, essentially demonstrating greater value (like a more time-intensive and therefore "time-expensive" primary care visit) that may actually result in better care and less overall expense—fewer unnecessary tests and better coordination of care.

If insurers are serious about driving change in healthcare delivery they *need to take a leadership role in creating a new basis for payment.* Reduced treatment costs mean reduced revenue for providers and lower premiums for insurers. Beyond clearly unnecessary care, other reductions in medical treatment costs translate to lower revenues for physicians and hospitals. This challenge to their business models has to be addressed in some way to overcome resistance to change. But the challenge is not the insurer's alone. All market factors point to lower reimbursement rates and more restrictive access.[2]

If medical treatment costs drop significantly, under PPACA rules today, insurers would have to lower health plan premiums to stay in compliance with medical loss ratio (MLR) minimums. A reduction in the volume of claims may or may not mean any savings in administrative costs for a given insurer. One opportunity rests in dramatically improved efficiency through new payment approaches that address *outcomes* rather than volume and specific codes for given procedures.

The trend is toward further commoditization of health plans, *so insurers must leverage their networks as a source of differentiation.* A key challenge for any commercial payer is whether it can turn its network into an asset and competitive differentiator with qualities beyond breadth such as overall efficiency or overall higher quality of care. Those payers that can engage in closer collaboration with providers will build network loyalty, minimizing disruption for its employer customers and their employees and reducing internal costs related to network churn.

What Payers Can Do

In light of all the recent healthcare changes, many insurers have developed a range of initiatives to develop more strategic relationships with providers, in other words, hospital systems and independent physician practices. The goal of these initiatives is to generate better health outcomes at lower cost. One of the problems is that most insurers have attempted to do this incrementally within the existing business model. This approach, while it makes sense on one level—because it's a continuation of what's been done—is guaranteed not to work because it's a continuation of the current business model.

To really change things, in other words, create better health outcomes at lower cost, the approach has to take a continuum of care approach over a broader time horizon than what has been previously considered. Yet, if we introduce change but we don't address the underlying causes of inefficiency, duplication, and error, we won't solve the problem!

Let's take the case of a healthcare delivery client that's trying to negotiate a bundled price with payers and employers on a direct basis. They are interested in, willing, and able to create a predictive price and assume risk. They've defined comprehensively what will be included with deliverables and metrics on the back end. Employers—who care about their employees—are very excited and open to this model. But if the next conversation is with a benefits person on the employer side, then they find themselves back in the old model because the benefits person doesn't know what to do with this "exception."

To move to a different model, there has to be a bridge from the executive who's interested in introducing a new model to the people who operationally execute agreements with providers. The same dynamic occurs between providers and insurers. At the strategy level, executives are interested in new payment models—defining and paying for care differently—but where claims get adjudicated, the systems are already set up and people are incented to perform in the old model, in other words, we can't/won't process exceptions.

So what are insurers doing as we move to bundled payments? Some insurers define bundled payments and risk-sharing with providers as a roll-up of all the Current Procedural Terminology (CPT) codes that are used today with a total reduced cost—essentially putting the risk back on the provider—an approach in other words unlikely to get much traction on the provider side. On the other hand, insurers are understandably wary and would be ill advised to create a blank check and hand it over to a provider. Insurers have been concerned with the practice of upcoding and unnecessary utilization that has lined providers' pockets for years.

So, what's the solution here? Clearly, any solution requires the development of partnerships with selected providers who are able to bring innovation and accountability for outcomes and who are also willing to accept payment outside the typical adjudication system. To create the necessary infrastructure, insurers will need to step out of their silos and the usual method of doing business. They'll need to think through and identify exceptions and then define how they'll address them, probably doing "work arounds" in order to prove the concept before any system redesign.

Develop Partnerships with Providers

During the course of our work with insurers, we've run into some common themes as insurers structure strategic initiatives and operationalize systems to support them. While many of the initiatives in recent years have been designed to encourage providers to make desired changes in business process and care delivery (primarily to drive down costs), many insurers have failed to adequately engage providers in the change process. Doing so requires an understanding of what providers value and then finding ways to make those elements part of the deal. Since success is so dependent on the ability of network providers to change the way they deliver care, insurers will need to provide more structure for providers in order to ensure positive outcomes.

Historically, insurers have not been successful in driving change through providers, so doing "what we've always done" is not a solution! If providers agree to adopt performance-based contracts and fail, they are likely to demand a return to annual escalators. Insurers need to review their network strategies to ensure they are driving the *right* outcomes and addressing the needs of *all* stakeholders impacted.

Segment Providers

Insurers need to recognize that any initiatives they undertake will only add value if they are implemented successfully, and at the end of the day, generate better health outcomes at lower cost. Targeting or segmenting network providers to identify those that are most likely to be successful with a given initiative and then concentrating resources on that group will be critical to forward progress. In turn, successful implementation will help to sell other providers on the approach while generating positive clinical and financial outcomes. As noted earlier, insurers are at risk if providers don't implement change initiatives well, and if quality isn't improved, costs won't be lowered.

Insurers need to move away from broadly offering initiatives to the entire range of providers. Instead, they need to segment or qualify providers based on their ability to implement cost and quality improvements effectively and then only promote initiatives to those with the highest potential to succeed. Payer-driven initiatives should be realistic in scope, bearing in mind the support needs and limited change management capabilities of most healthcare organizations. Specific safety initiatives or 30-day readmissions, which have CMS sanctions pending, would be obvious candidates. Better to succeed with more modest goals than to have the provider fail to meet its objectives in a more ambitious context.

Focus Partnerships on the Prevention of Never Events

Historically, CMS has been weak at enforcing policies around never events. But the country's largest payer is recognizing that this is an area of significant cost savings. After all, in what other industry do we pay companies to fix problems that shouldn't have occurred in the first place? Private insurers also have a lot to gain if never events are reduced and are in a great position to support hospitals with their efforts to comply with the new rules. Once never events are reduced significantly, insurers would be in a great position to enforce strict denial of claims rules with reduced risk of losing providers from their network. They could also take a very public stance on not reimbursing for never events.

Require and Pay for Predictive Care Paths

While some health conditions are clearly too complex and variable to map a treatment path, in other words not true for all conditions. Leading healthcare providers such as Geisinger Health System, Gundersen Lutheran Health System, Mayo Clinic, and Sutter Health have already done considerable research establishing predictive care paths. This is an example of evidence-based medicine at work. It is now generally understood that the amount and types of care required for some conditions can be anticipated. Therefore, a total cost for treatment can be established without creating an added administrative cost burden by boring down into step-by-step detail and paying separately for those component parts.[3–8] In the area of cancer care, Cancer Treatment Centers of America has taken the lead in providing a comprehensive, integrated diagnostic evaluation and treatment plan for the four major types of cancer (i.e., breast, colorectal, prostate, and lung) for a fixed fee and in five days or less. They are poised to provide treatment for selected cancers on a fully transparent, bundled price basis.

Predictive care paths, and the outcomes they achieve, are the true "product" of hospitals and physicians, not each procedural detail. Considering the goals of healthcare reform, this implies that, like manufacturers, investments in "R&D" (e.g., new approaches to care delivery) will need to become part of the new business model. Differential pricing is then based on the quality of outcomes produced. As such, these "products" can be audited for quality just as products of pharmaceutical and medical device manufacturers are audited. This addresses one of the biggest disconnects of fee-for-service and capitation[9] payment methods—*they do nothing to ensure quality of care*. Care paths as a tangible product of evidence-based medicine also promise a better standard of care than the Joint Commission on the Accreditation of Healthcare Organizations (JCAHO), which continues to accredit hospitals that other sources say are unsafe. Innovations in healthcare delivery should lower costs and improve outcomes, as is true in other industries.

With a fixed total price for an evidence-based course of treatment associated with outcomes, there is no incentive to provide additional, unnecessary care. Significant administrative efficiency can also be achieved, moving away from the cost-accounting minutiae of the current system, which consumes provider time and encourages upcoding abuse.

As "products," there must also be transparency of both the price and the value of the care path products being offered. Responsible buyers need this information if we expect them to be accountable for the cost consequences of their decisions. This is true of CMS, private insurance, or consumer buyers. Transparency of price and value is already evident and established in elective healthcare markets such as cosmetic dermatology and corrective vision surgery. There's no reason why such practices can't successfully be extended to the broader range of high-volume treatments.

Change the Basis for Paying Primary Care Physicians

At the same time we are recognizing the importance of primary care in prevention and managing health to avoid more costly care, we are facing a critical shortage of primary care physicians. The reason for this is how we pay these physicians today. Their average compensation is so much less than subspecialists who perform procedures that are more richly compensated that we have eliminated any incentive to practice primary care. This is now widely recognized as one of the most important issues payment reform must address.[3,5,10,11,12]

Primary care takes time with a patient—to ask questions and diagnose the root cause behind symptoms, to study diagnostic tests and patient history, to educate patients and guide them in managing their own health, and to coordinate their care when subspecialists need to be involved. As such, *the important unit of value for primary care physicians is time*.

We can establish a dollar value for an hour of a primary care physician's time, and we can adjust this regionally based on cost-of-living data. This eliminates the incentive to minimize time with patients in order to see as many patients as possible, which is what these physicians need to do today to sustain an income. This value must also be set at a level that eliminates the disincentive to choose primary care practice. The 5–10% pay increases outlined in the PPACA legislation don't come close to adequately addressing the current compensation disparity between primary care and subspecialty practice.

Insurers, including CMS, can periodically audit physician practices, focusing on outlier time charges. If there is a trend of such outlier practice, without any supporting rationale, insurers can choose to exit such physicians from their networks. In addition, patients can fill out *standard of care report cards*, which would verify that the care that should be delivered was in fact delivered—in effect measuring how well a physician used their time with the patient.

Just as we defined a predictive care path as a product, so too is primary care management. Changing the unit of value to time doesn't remove the requirement for *price and value transparency* of primary physician care. For example, there *will* be primary care physicians who achieve better results over a continuum in helping their patients manage diabetes or obesity.

Buyers—consumers or insurers—can only make responsible choices when the price and value are known. Concierge primary care has already established the precedent for a known product (ready access to the physician) and a corresponding price.

Today, physicians are in an insurer's network because they have agreed to accept that payer's discounted schedule of charges. The physician then determines how to play the coding game to get more money. We're suffering from the consequences of this payment approach. Our proposal for tomorrow provides for fair, time-based compensation to physicians and kicks them out of the network if audits and patient standard of care report cards indicate they are "working the system."

Appropriate valuing of primary care and rebalancing compensation accordingly is a two-edged sword. Just as we are substantially underpaying for primary care, we are correspondingly overcompensating surgeons and subspecialists. Our redesign of financing mechanisms must address compensation imbalance *from both directions*. To be direct, this strategy calls for the relative reduction of subspecialist compensation as primary care compensation would increase.

Over time, the natural law of supply and demand will result in more primary care physicians and fewer subspecialists. As we've suggested, removing the income disincentive to choose the practice of primary care will change the ratio of primary care to subspecialists. This, and the impact of better primary care in avoiding surgery and specialist work, and thus reducing demand, will also result in reducing the number of subspecialists.

Increase Consumer Engagement and Personal Responsibility, Reducing the Abuse of the System by Consumers

We are currently paying avoidable healthcare costs due to two types of abuse by consumers. One is not managing their own health, and the other is not buying any type of insurance coverage even if they are able to afford it.

A necessary part of this strategy is the need to accept the reality that some people will always get away with "working the system." Regardless, significantly reducing the number of abusers of the system represents tremendous cost savings and collectively better health.

Reduce Fraud and Abuse by Providers

Private insurers on average do a reasonable job of verifying claims, monitoring trends, and taking actions to identify and address fraud. Their for-profit, bottom-line orientation drives them to perform this work, a responsibility of any organization buying products or services. This is the point where payment for services that are appropriately, actually, and satisfactorily rendered should always be determined.

CMS doesn't currently operate at this same standard, a point argued clearly in a series of essays by industry experts in "Stop Paying the Crooks."[14] Merrill and Meredith Matthews note the irony that the Medicare program is held up by some as the model for healthcare in this country.[15] In 2008, Senator Charles Grassley pegged Medicare fraud, waste, and abuse at approximately $60 billion annually out of an annual budget of $460 billion—essentially 13%.[16] To put this all in perspective, Bernard Madoff ran a Ponzi scheme bilking customers out of some $50 billion, which appropriately set off a firestorm across the country. Madoff's transgressions were a one-time event; Medicare's losses to fraud, waste, and abuse are annual. Fraud can be immediately and substantively reduced by CMS adopting private insurers' best practices in this area. In fact, the Secretary of the US Department of Health and Human Services (HHS), Kathleen Sebelius, recently announced fraud prevention efforts that netted the government $4.1 billion in 2011.

Are You Ready for Disruptive Innovation?

Private health insurance stands on the precipice of an uncertain future. After decades of financial success, it's difficult for many in the industry to think about meaningfully changing the current model. Yet no business model continues to deliver results into perpetuity. When market realities change, so must the model—and market realities have definitely changed.

Now, even the biggest employers are facing unprecedented cost pressures. Where they once valued premium-priced medical management tools and services, their insurer selection has quickly devolved to shopping on price. As a result, margins are eroding, and once secure customer relationships can no longer be counted on in the next sales forecast.

As we noted earlier, on the nonmarket side, many in government are intent on driving healthcare reform through increased government intervention to control insurance costs. This comes on top of the fact that over half of insured Americans get their insurance from the government (Medicaid and Medicare).

Many healthcare insurers feel vulnerable, and rightfully so. Conducting business as usual won't cut it in a future in other words undergoing radical change now and continuing through 2014. Recognizing the need for a fundamentally new business model is a necessary first step to change. Developing such a model is the more difficult challenge that lies ahead.

Underlying the obvious perils facing private healthcare insurers are some potentially potent opportunities to make disruptive changes and seize substantial market share. Leaders throughout the industry need to be proactive in initiating business model innovation and guiding its effective implementation. Throughout the industry, new winners—and losers—will emerge based on their ability to design and deliver superior economic and health outcome value. Are you ready for that contest?

Endnotes

1. "Adapting to the Changing Landscape of Healthcare Insurance" by Rita E. Numerof and Bill Ott, last modified October 29, 2009, http://www.nai-consulting.com/files/pdf/articles/191.pdf.
2. "Healthcare Reform: Strategy, Myths and Solutions," by Rita E. Numerof, *Medical Progress Today*, November 13, 2009, http://www.medicalprogresstoday.com/spotlight/spotlight_indarchive.php?id=1830.
3. Lola Butcher, "Bundled Payments: Brilliant Idea or Boondoggle?" *Physician Executive* July/August 2009, 35(4): 6–8,10. http://net.acpe.org/MembersOnly/pejournal/2009/JulyAugust/Butcher.pdf.
4. Francois de Brantes, Meredith B. Rosenthal, and Michael Painter, "Building a Bridge from Fragmentation to Accountability: The Prometheus Payment," *New England Journal of Medicine*, 361, no. 11 (2009):1033–1036, http://content.nejm.org/cgi/content/full/NEJMp0906121.
5. Tom Doerr, Randy Bak, Frank Ingari, and Debra Gribble. *The Collaborative Payer Model: New Hope for Medicare and Primary Care*, November 24, 2008, ESSENCE Healthcare, http://www.essencecorp.com/pdf/ExecutiveSummary_CPM.pdf.
6. Harold D. Miller, "From Volume to Value: Better Ways to Pay for Health Care," September/October 2009, Health Affairs, http://content.healthaffairs.org/cgi/content/abstract/28/5/1418.
7. Arnold Milstein "Medical Homes—And Medical 'Home Runs'?" September 10, 2008, Health Affairs, http://healthaffairs.org/blog/2008/09/10/medical-homes-and-medical-home-runs/.
8. Anne Underwood, *Prescriptions: The Business of Health Care* blog, "A New Way to Pay Physicians," interview with Dr. John C. Lewin, September 23, 2009, *New York Times* online, http://prescriptions.blogs.nytimes.com/2009/09/23/a-new-way-to-pay-physicians/.
9. Capitation is a payment method that pays a fixed fee to serve a patient population. When established in the 1980s, there was no measurement or requirement for quality of care. As such, the incentive was for providers to maximize profit by minimizing the health services they provided.

10. American Board of Medical Specialties, Specialties and Subspecialties: Recognized Physician Specialty and Subspecialty Certificates" (n.d.), http://www.abms.org/who_we_help/physicians/specialties.aspx (accessed May 4, 2012).

11. Blue Cross Blue Shield Association, *BCBSA Recommendations for Expanding Primary Care Access* (Washington, DC: Blue Cross Blue Shield Association, September 2009).

12. Thomas Bodenheimer, Robert A.Berenson, and Paul Rudolf, "The Primary Care–Specialty Income Gap: Why It Matters," *Annals of Internal Medicine*, Volume 146, no. 4(2007): 301–306, http://www.annals.org/cgi/content/abstract/146/4/301.

13. James R. Frogue and Newt Gingrich, "Stop Paying the Crooks," Center for Health Transformation, 2009, CHT Press, September 2009.

14. Merrill Matthews and Meredith R. Matthews. "Medicare Fraud: What the Government Can Learn from the Private Sector," 2009; Frogue and Gingrich, "Stop Paying the Crooks," 79–98. Center for Health Transformation. CHT Press, September 2009.

15. Matthews and Matthews, "Medicare Fraud," Frogue and Gingrich, "Stop Paying the Crooks," 84. Center for Health Transformation, CHT Press, September 2009.

Chapter 7

Big Pharma: How to Regain Success

Successful companies, even entire industries, have a lifecycle. All of them eventually reach the point where their business model approaches the end of its lifecycle and is no longer viable. Companies that recognize the shift early on, assuming they execute the successor model effectively, become leaders as the next stage emerges. Sometimes the transitions are incremental and gradual; more often, they involve discontinuity and dislocation. Outlines of the transition are always clear in retrospect, and most of our wisdom about such transitions comes from retrospective analysis. But what's the appropriate advice for companies in the middle of a transition—when the old model still appears to have life and the new model is underdeveloped and unproven?

The global pharmaceutical industry faces this situation today. It's well known that pharma's been going through tough times. It's now fashionable among politicians, pundits, and journalists to criticize all the ways in which the industry's pursuit of profit conflicts with the healthcare needs of patients. The industry has had to bear greater scrutiny and skepticism from all its stakeholders than it has known for decades. The tangible impact has taken the form of patient lawsuits, governmental investigations, increasingly aggressive efforts of third-party payers to influence pricing and utilization of branded drugs, a more cautious approach to clinical evidence and new drug approval on the part of regulators, and new constraints on sales and marketing practices.

These very serious challenges are reflected in the valuations that investors give pharmaceutical companies. For example, as of February 2012, the Nasdaq Pharmaceutical Index remained about 15% below the levels of March 2001. At the same time, it's fair to say that the reality beneath the headlines may be a lot more positive.

Given the rapid progress of medical science and the huge swaths of unmet medical needs that remain, the opportunity for innovation is undiminished. Big pharma is still the natural champion for bringing safe and cost-effective therapies to the market on a global scale, and it continues to possess enormous competitive advantages in that role. At the end of the day, no one else can muster the critical competencies on the necessary scale to bring new medical therapies to market on a consistent basis.

To some extent, the industry has been unfairly maligned. It's a more convenient target of criticism than current dysfunctional systems for delivering and paying for medical care. It's also the victim of limited understanding of the realities of medical science and healthcare economics among the general population—the inherent trade-offs involved between innovation and short-term cost, between short-term cost of preventive care and long-term cost of acute and long-term care, and among the various combinations of efficacy and safety that all treatments (or nontreatments) involve.

On the basis of these underlying strengths, one could argue that the current problems are temporary and that the industry's primary imperative is to become more effective at public diplomacy. In our view, this conclusion is the wrong one for the industry to make. Healthcare delivery models are undergoing a sea change. Rising costs will force us to change the way we look at healthcare. Over time, we will embrace the concept of a continuum of care that emphasizes prevention and more active engagement of consumers in their own treatment, not unlike the model being adopted in the treatment of diabetes.

Unfortunately, the pathway to get there will almost certainly involve more short-sighted and heavy-handed attempts to control costs. It's imperative for major pharmaceutical companies to become active participants in shaping public policy and the public's attitudes toward it. At the same time, there are very real problems with the current pharma business model. Leaders of pharma companies should seize this opportunity to conduct a fundamental self-examination and begin laying the foundation for their future.

Vulnerabilities of the Current Model

The dominant business model for the pharmaceutical industry today has been the blockbuster model.[1] In its simplest terms, the blockbuster model is about:

- focusing development investments on drugs that address large patient populations and appeal to a broad prescriber base;
- achieving high penetration of those markets through aggressive and expensive promotional activities to physicians and patients; and
- expanding market boundaries by pursuing new indications and broadening the prescriber base beyond the initially targeted specialists.

The remarkable success of some blockbuster products has reinforced each of these elements. At the same time, the inherent costs and risks of the model have encouraged company mergers on a mammoth scale and reinforced the barriers to entry into this elite club of global companies. All elements of the model continue to operate, but under increasing strain, due to some fundamental vulnerabilities.

The first vulnerability reflects the model's dependence on mass markets. The larger the target audience is, the greater the likelihood that some segment of it will respond negatively to the product in question. Legal liability and societal backlash are likewise proportional to market size. In response to recent recalls of major products, the reaction of key stakeholders has been to emphasize safety as an overriding concern. The perception that big pharma has not been sufficiently sensitive to this issue has hurt the industry's reputation, and it also translates into an escalating regulatory burden on the industry.

The second vulnerability surrounds significant costs in an increasingly cost-conscious market. The model is very expensive and requires three major cost drivers that continue to trend higher: discovery or acquisition of promising compounds, development through human trials, and marketing of approved drugs. Historically, companies have been able to recoup their investments and generate an attractive return by pricing their products based on efficacy and safety, with only limited attention to the prices for competitive therapies or no therapy.

These escalating costs, passed through to payers, are in direct conflict with a growing urgency in the United States and elsewhere in the developed world to control the accelerating cost of healthcare. Payers have some powerful tools at their disposal in this conflict. The greatest of these is the accumulation of existing therapies that are off patent or approaching patent expiration. As it has become easier to bring generic drugs to market, their overwhelming cost advantages have provided powerful incentives to payers and pharmacists to promote substitution. Even within the world of branded pharmaceuticals, the proliferation of compounds with similar properties makes it easier for payers to force greater price competition by granting preferential formulary status to selected brands. In a sense, the very advantage of many block-buster products—that they address broad markets—has been turned against them.

The third vulnerability of the model is that it depends on mass messaging. In the past era of limited price sensitivity, competition was based on companies' ability to convey messages about features and benefits to physicians and patients. In this game, reach and frequency were the critical metrics. As companies have increased the frequency of their messaging, the market has become saturated with physician detailing and direct-to-customer (DTC) advertising. Beyond providing basic familiarity, the messages themselves tend to be low-value-added to their audiences. Not surprisingly, there is growing resistance—to the point of backlash—to this approach to marketing.

The traditional product-driven model often fails to take into account broader market needs or issues. For example, the traditional approach fails to ask a number of questions critical in today's market, like:

- Is there evidence that the product is better than what is currently on the market?
- Will payers and physicians be interested without evidence of superior clinical outcomes even at the same price?
- Will providers buy the product (at a premium) if it is only as good as current products?
- What evidence of improved outcomes or lower treatment costs will payers want in order to accept the product?

Market-Driven Business Model

Inherent limitations of the current business model will lead to the emergence of a fundamentally new approach for the industry that addresses the needs and interests of all critical stakeholders. This market-driven model rests on the following assumption: successful companies of the future will determine what therapeutic areas they will "own," which in turn will drive investments. Unlike the current approach, which is really *product* centric, the new model will be *patient* centric and take a *continuum of care versus episodic care* approach. What this will mean is a core focus on prevention, diagnosis, and treatment of the range of conditions within a therapeutic area, taking into account the needs of specific markets around the globe.

At the same time, companies increasingly must be able to demonstrate the economic and clinical value (or ECV) of their products. This paradigm shift requires that marketing strategies focus on the market needs (pull), instead of pushing a particular product (push). The market-driven model can be characterized by its focus on delivering real value to stakeholders, strategic marketing, and innovation. The market is a good indicator of when market forces are working. Take a look at Avastin®—even before the Food and Drug Administration (FDA) removed its indication for breast cancer, the market had responded to postapproval studies, as indicated by the fact that use of the drug for treating metastatic breast cancer had plummeted as more data about its limitations became available.

Ensuring Stakeholder Value

The central imperative of the new model is delivering real value to *all* stakeholders—payers, regulators, physicians, providers, and patients. And understanding whose voice matters in terms of relative weight is of critical importance.

Globally, the power of payers is growing as product acceptance and purchase decision making moves further and further from the physician. Payers and hospitals are clamping down on healthcare costs by saying no to new products, line extensions, and of course, price increases. Reacting to the prospect of exponentially increasing liabilities, payers of all types are demanding hard comparative clinical and economic data to justify any change with bottom-line impact. Historically, market access was considered a reimbursement issue that was given attention late in the product development process. Yet, as pressure on payers and providers to reduce costs and increase quality grows, pharmaceutical manufacturers must understand who the stakeholders are—patients, providers, and payers—and build relevant data to demonstrate their value to each one. Consequently, manufacturers must think about market access considerations much earlier in the product development process.

This represents a significant change for many companies. Those tasked with Marketing Products are beginning to recognize the internal challenges they face in gaining acceptance for market access considerations, specifically, the need for comparative effectiveness research (CER) and the identification of new ways of obtaining appropriate evidence. They are increasingly seeking help with translating these messages internally and implementing sustainable changes within their companies.

The FDA and other regulators also remain a critical constituency. Companies need to find ways to accelerate time-to-market while reducing clinical trial costs and attaining optimal claims. Clinical and regulatory affairs groups will need to hone their capabilities for early and effective engagement of regulators to influence regulatory thinking, avoid surprises, and develop well-defined clinical strategies to ensure that the right studies are conducted in the right order to minimize delays and rework.

Payers have emerged in recent years as the newest powerful constituency. Pharmaceutical companies need to engage with governments, employers, and insurers to understand their needs, deliver solutions that address those needs, and frame the discussion over healthcare economics more advantageously. To accomplish this, several significant changes to the current process will be required. First, healthcare economics considerations need to move to the front end of the product development and investment prioritization cycle. Second, clinical trials need to be structured to demonstrate compelling clinical and economic value in comparison with available alternatives; and finally, the engagement of payer organizations needs to be managed as a complex selling process.

Perhaps most importantly, companies need to change their go-to-market models—redefining the value delivered to physicians, providers, and patients—while lowering costs. The heavy reliance on physician detailing is inconsistent with cost constraints and the need for more tailored and responsive dialogue. The role of personal promotion to physicians hasn't disappeared, but it requires greater sophistication, clinical knowledge, and business acumen than typical sales reps possess today in order to engage in the kind of meaningful conversations that physicians would truly value. Current technology will also play a role in getting information out to key constituents. Companies will need to define new approaches and develop new competencies to deliver value in ways that are cost effective, convenient, and tailored to meet individual needs. In addition, opportunities to develop relationships with patients/consumers need to be part of the equation as well.

Strategic Marketing Capabilities

One of the insidious characteristics of the blockbuster model is that it is inherently product driven. Insiders at even the largest global pharmaceutical companies can name the blockbuster products that drive business strategy for the company. Because product revenues are so central to the companies' success, they also tend to be sales-driven cultures. All pharmaceutical companies invest in marketing capabilities, but these groups typically have too tactical a focus. In practice, marketing operates largely as a sales support organization.

In the market-driven model, strategic marketing drives all other activities, and sales are repositioned as just one arm of the marketing mix. The central premise (and promise) of the model is that better understanding of, and responsiveness to, the needs of all stakeholders will enable companies to better identify and define unmet medical needs, determine therapeutic focus to drive disciplined portfolio investment decisions, deliver appropriate new therapies and ancillary services, and capture sufficient value for their products. This promise can only be realized if companies invest in the capabilities of strategic marketing. Marketing in other words truly strategic involves segmentation of markets based on characteristics that correlate with distinctive needs. It also requires a level of insight that goes well beyond the standard specialty- and decile-driven approaches in common use today.

Innovation Stewardship

Innovation remains the lifeblood of major pharmaceutical companies. Pharmaceutical innovation is inherently high risk, expensive, part science, part art. But these attributes are magnified in the blockbuster model, which focuses on indications and molecules that have the revenue potential to sustain the commercial infrastructure of the company.

In the new model, companies will use marketing insights to determine therapeutic focus and drive disciplined portfolio investment decisions that reflect a more holistic view of product lifecycle value and the continuum of care. Once companies move to a market model with a more efficient and effective commercial arm, they can focus more resources on research and development (R&D) in those therapeutic areas that strategic marketing has determined to represent the greatest opportunities for the company.

Along with this greater flexibility and focus, in a more cost-conscious environment, companies also need to extract more value from their innovation activities. In their management of both early- and late-stage pipelines, they need to take a seamless, market-driven approach to selecting therapeutic targets. They also need to apply more flexible risk management and value-capture strategies, including greater use of out-licensing and co-development, to derive the greatest expected value from the pipeline. In their management of products toward the end of their lifecycles, companies need to become more aggressive at pursuing exit strategies in order to focus resources on what big pharma does best—bringing novel therapies to market.

But they also need to think differently about their clinical research—the design and conduct of trials and the role of real-world evidence—especially as we look ahead to the possibility of real advances in personalized medicine and the role of theranostics.

Pressures on Innovation

Today, pharmaceutical and medical device manufacturers rely on patents to protect their innovations as they compete in commercial markets. In most cases, innovators have 17 years from the date of patent issuance to recoup their investment. But having a patent isn't the same as having a product. First you need Food and Drug Administration (FDA) approval if you plan to sell products in the United States.

That's when the real work begins. Experts estimate that it costs more than $1 billion and takes 10 years to bring a new drug to market. There are lots of patents sitting on the shelf, never to see the commercial light of day. Molecules may not perform the way scientists expected in the earliest stages of discovery; side effects may prove to be problematic, thus stopping development in the middle of clinical trials. And getting the biggest US insurer, the Centers for Medicare and Medicaid Services (CMS), to agree to reimburse the product is a further hurdle that must be crossed.

Given the substantial time and financial commitments required to bring a new drug to market, congressional and public pressure to further reduce the length of patent protection represents a major challenge for the US medical products industry. What most people don't realize is this very pressure puts at risk one of our few remaining industrial jewels. The argument put forth in support of more limited protection is the opportunity to bring generics to market faster and at a significantly lower cost than branded pharmaceuticals.

That generics come at a cheaper price shouldn't be a surprise to anyone. Generic manufacturers don't have to invest in risky R&D, don't bear the brunt of regulatory approval, and don't have the same commercialization costs to bear. But the focus on bringing generics out faster to lower overall healthcare costs misses one critical point. Pharmaceuticals, while highly visible, represent only about 10% of the cost of healthcare in the United States. And they enable greater productivity on the part of people taking them for the most part! If we're serious about lowering healthcare costs, then we need to look elsewhere.

Role of CER in the Pharmaceutical Industry

Earlier we discussed the impact of recent healthcare legislation on the overall industry. One component, CER, has had a major impact on the pharmaceutical and medical device industries. CER represents a significant shift for the industry and promises to radically alter the level of government involvement in the way healthcare products and services are developed; it is seen by CMS as *the* solution to healthcare cost containment.[2]

As we discussed in Chapter 4, CER is not restricted to research into what products work best; it also includes research into what *treatment protocols* work best. What this means is a fundamental restructuring of priorities within large segments of the industry, away from incremental improvements (i.e., formula modification, extended release) and toward improvements that are of interest to payers, patients, and providers. There are as likely to be demands to reduce cost as there are for *quality improvements*. This will put significant pressure on pharmaceutical manufacturers to produce products that demonstrate *substantial* improvements in outcomes.

Given that pharmaceuticals are a very visible portion of those expenditures, they are likely to be among the first targets of CER. Primarily, we expect that this will take the form of comparisons between drugs, classes of drugs, especially where there is controversy regarding the relative benefits of older (generic) drugs and newer, branded ones, and even non-interventional approaches (e.g., watchful waiting) will increase. Branded pharmaceuticals are still the targets of choice for political purposes, but biologics may be close behind, especially given their often extremely high costs. These pressures will come in the form of treatment guidelines, focus on cost effectiveness, and the end of the placebo-controlled trial. In addition, the development of companion targeted diagnostics that identify appropriate patients and reduce side effects will become increasingly important.

Treatment Guidelines

Looking down the road a few years, there will almost certainly be relatively stringent guidelines for the treatment of the most expensive medical conditions, including what drugs to prescribe and under what circumstances.

Because of the objection of the American Medical Association (AMA) and other powerful lobbies to the outright restriction of physician prerogatives in choosing a treatment, there are likely to be exceptions to these guidelines. But given the march of physicians to employment models, coupled with downward reimbursement pressure on healthcare systems and their need to reduce costs significantly, standardized clinical protocols based on available evidence will surely characterize the landscape of the future.

In the long term, we expect that compliance will be strong, especially as retail providers (e.g., Walmart and Walgreens) enter the primary care delivery space. What's more, once these specific treatment patterns become the standard, they will (a) be adopted by most private insurers (some of whom are actively buying delivery organizations), and (b) be adopted by physicians themselves as the default standard of treatment. This will create a high degree of conformity. *Those drugs not baked into protocols and treatment guidelines will have a tough time surviving!*

Conditions most likely to be targeted by CER:

1. Cardiovascular conditions, including stroke, ischemic heart disease, congestive heart failure, atherosclerosis, and hypertension. Finding the most cost-effective preventives and treatments will be a priority. The cost effectiveness of drugs versus angioplasty and stenting will be evaluated, as will the effectiveness of branded versus generic drugs.
2. Type 2 diabetes prevention and treatment. Expect comparison of weight loss interventions like exercise and bariatric surgery versus drugs and combination therapies that include drugs, as well as evaluation of various predictive screening regimens and alternative points of intervention during the progression of the disease. Expect this research to focus heavily on the potential for differential effectiveness across specific subpopulations.
3. Obesity. Expect comparison of weight-loss interventions, including reevaluation of the safety and benefits of older drugs for weight loss, as well as the relative advantages of drugs versus bariatric surgery.
4. Cancer. Research priorities in this area are likely to revolve around the relative effectiveness of various drug and radiation regimens, and attempts to segment the clinical population to prescribe the most effective drugs based on diagnostic and genetic testing. This has the potential to evolve into a strict set of segmentation criteria that allows more precise, data-based prescribing and narrower indications for in-market drugs.
5. Neurological Disorders, including Alzheimer's and other forms of senile dementia. The cost effectiveness of current drugs for treating Alzheimer's disease and Parkinson's disease will be called into question, as will classes of drugs that are, cumulatively, very expensive (e.g., antidepressants).
6. Arthritis and joint problems. Especially given recent findings that some procedures (e.g., lavage and debridement) are ineffective in

most cases and the high cost and frequency of joint replacement, evaluating whether nonsurgical approaches are effective will be a high priority.

7. Respiratory illness. Pneumonia will make the list, and we think it is likely to be combined with influenza as part of a respiratory illness priority area. Treatment protocols and prevention of nosocomial infections are likely to be focus areas.

8. Chronic obstructive pulmonary disorder will make the list, and research will focus on the relative effectiveness and cost of various treatment protocols.

9. HIV/AIDS is likely to make the list of priorities, not so much because there is controversy regarding the relative clinical or cost effectiveness of current treatment regimens, but because it would be politically imprudent not to name it to a list of federal research priorities.

Companies gaining a large portion of their revenues or profits from drugs used in *priority areas,* such as in the treatment of cardiovascular disease, mental health (especially Alzheimer's disease and depression), as well as those heavily invested in rapidly growing areas such as gastroesophageal reflux disease (GERD) and dyspepsia are most at risk. We should note, however, that they also stand to gain the most should their products be the ultimate "winners," in other words, they should be selected by CMS as the first-line treatment for people suffering from these conditions.

Focus on Cost Effectiveness

The focus on cost effectiveness reflected in the funding of CER places an increased burden on pharmaceutical companies to preemptively evaluate the likely value of their products. Economic and clinical value considerations will have to be an integral part of R&D and clinical trials work.

In that context, it's imperative that major pharmaceutical companies focus on creating products of real marginal value to patients, providers, and payers. In many cases, this requires rethinking the approach to discovery and development in

ways that increase the probability and frequency of successful new drugs. As with any change in approach, ensuring
adoption will also require modifying the organizational context—the roles, accountabilities, compliance practices, and
incentives—to ensure compliance with the new approach.

End of the Placebo-Only Controlled Trial

Placebo-only controlled trials will no longer be acceptable to
CMS unless there are no other treatments available for a given
condition, because the data they create is nearly worthless
for comparative effectiveness purposes. For cost-effectiveness
evaluation, the ideal is a direct head-to-head trial against whatever drug would be supplanted by the new one (e.g., against
the current first-line treatment if the new drug is projected to
become the new first-line treatment; against the current second-
line treatment if it's projected to become the new second-line
treatment). This greatly increases the risk of bringing a new
compound to market, because a "lost" comparison may exclude
the drug from the market or relegate it to very marginal status.

We expect that placebo-only controlled trials will be insuf-
ficient for obtaining coverage within three years, yet sufficient
for the determination to be made and "fair warning" to be
given. Drugs currently in phase I or II are likely to be subject
to new requirements.

Impact of CER on Pharmaceutical Operations

The most glaring impact of defined treatment guidelines and
cost effectiveness will be the immediate obsolescence of the
standard *frequency and coverage*, detailing-based sales model.
With a set of guidelines in place that specifies what drugs
will be prescribed for whom (under penalty of nonreimburse-
ment for their patients and possibly for themselves), the ability
to change physician behavior through education efforts (and
hence the return on sales efforts) will be greatly reduced.

This doesn't necessarily mean that detailing will be completely dead, but it will be limited to specific providers that have shown willingness to buck the reimbursement-led paradigm either by laboriously justifying exceptions or by catering to patients who are willing to pay out of pocket for premium drugs. Nevertheless, the optimal size of the sales force will be drastically reduced.

The need to take economic and clinical value considerations into account early in the process will require a redefinition of the role of research scientists, as well as the development of new competencies among these scientists and their managers. Health economics groups are likely to become integrated into marketing, because the need to *build* the economic and clinical value case and the need to *explain* it to multiple constituencies will become increasingly intertwined.

This redefined marketing group will also need to be closely integrated with R&D and clinical research, so that the expected cost effectiveness of a potential product, relative to existing treatments and those in development, can be assessed on an ongoing basis. What many in the industry fail to appreciate is that going forward, demonstration of cost-effective superior outcomes will be table stakes for reimbursement. Competition from generics will accelerate, and with the introduction of biosimilars over the next several years, the biologics sector—historically immune from such competition—will experience significant pain, just like pharmaceutical companies.

Changing behavior to be consistent with this approach will require a new kind of organizational infrastructure—one that clearly defines the roles of various parties to be consistent with the new organizational reality, ensures that those roles are adopted, and creates seamless collaboration across functional areas. The problem is not as simple as creating the new plan for collaborative research or presenting R&D with a new prioritization scheme. It also requires creating the infrastructure to ensure accountability and develop new competencies. The need to correctly define the positioning of a new product within treatment guidelines prior to conducting clinical trials will require deeper up-front analysis of the potential risks and benefits of various evidence generation strategies. It also suggests that a *rolling blockbuster* model may be appropriate. This is discussed in more detail in the next section, "Prudent Responses and Defensive Strategies." The difficulty and time required to accomplish this should not be underestimated.

The increased focus on cost effectiveness began several years ago, but the trend toward using it as a criterion for reimbursement will accelerate over the next few years. Drugs that are in R&D today are very likely to be launched into a market that explicitly issues guidelines on the basis of cost effectiveness. Consideration of economic and clinical value must be integrated into the entire product development and commercialization process, and this will not happen overnight.

Prudent Responses and Defensive Strategies

Several years ago we recommended that pharmaceutical companies would be wise to pursue three key defensive responses: develop service wraps, diversify revenue streams away from payers, and adopt a rolling blockbuster approach. We stand by these recommendations.

Develop Service Wraps

There are opportunities for pharmaceutical companies to increase the value of their offerings by bundling them with well-designed services. Use of a drug within a well-defined treatment protocol may enhance its value relative to other treatment options. To the extent that a specific service wrap becomes part of the standard of treatment, it creates an advantage in other words difficult for competitors to overcome. In order to successfully displace a wrapped service, a competitor would not only have to demonstrate superior cost effectiveness, but also sort out whether executing the existing protocol (or an alternative protocol) in conjunction with its product is more cost effective than the product alone. This may be more trouble and risk than a competitor is willing to take.

Of course, the only way to create initial support for the service wrap/drug combination is to demonstrate the same boost to cost effectiveness, so the added resistance to competition isn't free. It does have its benefits, however. A drug's patent may be several years old by the time it's ready to come to market, but a service wrap/treatment protocol that accompanies it will be protected from the time it's finalized. Just as surgical protocols are subject to intellectual property (IP) protection (allowing surgeons to collect licensing fees for the use of the protocol), service wraps that maximize the effectiveness of a pharmaceutical intervention are, too. This creates an extended revenue opportunity for the manufacturer.

It also means that hospital systems are more likely to be willing partners in the work of developing a protocol. They're also looking for ways to ensure that their "products" (their own treatment practices, especially those that are differentiated in some way from competitors) are recommended in the treatment guidelines and would be very happy to share in licensing revenues for the treatment protocol. With the growth of disease management companies, opportunities for strategic partnerships abound. Here, too, success will depend on the relative robustness of the economic and clinical evidence.

Diversify Revenue Streams Away from Payers

Effectively, this means refocusing development efforts on drugs that fall outside of the reimbursement system, in other words, lifestyle or premium drugs that consumers will pay for entirely, out of pocket. Entry into the lightly regulated (and almost entirely unreimbursed) nutritional market, where a pharmaceutical manufacturer's brand name can serve as assurance of the potency and purity of products, may also be a viable option.

It may also be possible to follow this path with customized medicine (e.g., using biomarkers to determine what treatment is most effective and appropriate). People may be willing to pay out of pocket for a drug in other words clearly indicated as appropriate specifically for them, even if insurers aren't willing to pay because the ECV evidence isn't sufficiently compelling from a payer perspective. In the same vein, pharmaceutical manufacturers may want to enter the market for diagnostic tests that identify those who are likely to benefit specifically from their drugs.

Even when these drugs pass economic and clinical criteria, they may still be controversial, as was the case when the National Health Service (NHS) fast-tracked approval for Herceptin®, and several NHS primary care trusts protested, saying they would have to cut other treatments to pay for it. The risk posed by this kind of dispute can be avoided to the extent that consumers come to accept that individual payment for individualized treatment is appropriate.

Adopt a Rolling Blockbuster Approach

The rolling blockbuster approach segments the market for a drug much more minutely than has historically been the case, creating a large number of target populations in which the drug's cost effectiveness can be assessed.[3] This reduces the risk inherent in clinical trials, because the binary outcome (reimbursed/not reimbursed) applies only for the small segment under consideration. For the population as a whole, it's the sum of those binary outcomes, which is a much more predictable outcome.

A second advantage of the approach is that it may make the drug a smaller target in the eyes of the cost-effectiveness hawks, as they would have to demonstrate its inferiority in a large number of diverse populations, each of which carries a relatively small price tag. The return for replacing the product with a more cost-effective one would be reduced.

The clear takeaway is that innovative companies that demonstrate the value of their products in this environment will flourish. Successful players will work to incorporate the needs of all stakeholders (payers, consumers/patients, physicians) into the product development process and generate new medicines that meet unmet needs and provide real value.

Those new products, by definition, won't face generic competition (at least not for a while) and will command top-tier prices.

The near-term pain comes from shifting from an old paradigm to the new paradigm. The old business rules, both at the FDA and in industry, focused on blockbuster products approved through large one-size-fits-all clinical trials need to change.

Some patients benefit more from specific products than others, some patients don't benefit at all, and some are even seriously harmed. Usually this last group is such a small number that in randomized clinical trials, it's considered noise. Given the enormous size of the patient groups treated, the net benefits of blockbuster drugs far outweighed their costs.

But recent and ongoing waves of blockbuster drug patent expirations are offering insurers cheap and very effective products. Rare side effects trumpeted in the media (like Vioxx®) have eroded regulators' willingness to approve drugs for primary care indications without prohibitively large and expensive clinical trials.

The blockbuster model that made billions for industry is putting itself out of business.

Instead of thinking big, innovators need to think small. If you shrink the denominator to just the segment of the market that genuinely benefits, then the value proposition for those small groups of targeted patients goes way up.

This approach builds on small niches of patients. *Nichebusters* like Gleevec® offer incredible outcomes to patients and profits to innovators. Taking a personalized medicine approach will allow companies to move from a *product-driven* model to one in other words truly *market driven*. Ironically, this model begins to resemble orphan drug development, which may, indeed, represent a shift in the R&D paradigm for the future.

The benefits of shifting focus to orphan drugs are many, including a streamlined approval process, patent extension and exclusivity, tax credits, and smaller clinical trials because of a narrow indication. Instead of looking at the population as everybody (let's say everybody with high cholesterol), you start looking at people with high cholesterol *and* a particular genetic profile. By targeting smaller, specific populations for disease management, companies get their product to market quicker and can reduce spending *without sacrificing innovation*.

The change in focus does come with its own set of challenges. As competition moves into the smaller spaces, everyone will be looking for an opportunity to get an *orphan drug designation* (ODD). This will likely lead to additional scrutiny and will intensify the need to demonstrate the economic and clinical value of your product as it applies to a particular population before approval. Shifting the R&D focus will require new capabilities across the entire business to meet these demands.

Despite some new challenges, the rewards can outweigh the risks. The overall cost of developing orphan drugs is typically less than that of other drugs. The paradigm shift even reaches beyond *just* R&D, since the smaller population doesn't require large marketing or promotional campaigns. Ultimately, the segmented approach enables drug companies to see competitive returns on investment, while increasing the value to the targeted market.

Interest in a new R&D paradigm is increasing, offering opportunity for the long term. Today's orphan drug could even become tomorrow's rolling blockbuster, a point not lost by Allergan in its support of the controversial drug, Botox®.

Real-World Example

In the late 1960s and early 1970s, Dr. Alan Scott, an ophthalmologist in San Francisco, investigated treatments for his patients who had crossed eyes (strabismus) and uncontrollable blinking (blepharospasm). He found one particular compound to be pretty successful at managing both these conditions and built a company, Oculinum, Inc., entirely around his new drug.[4]

Approved in 1984 as an orphan drug for uncontrolled blinking, neck pain, and muscle spasms, Oculinum treatment typically lasts about four to six months. As its use only relieved the chronic conditions temporarily, patients needed to come back to see the doctor two to three times a year, sometimes more, over a long period of time.

Around the same time that Dr. Scott's company received approval for Oculinum®, Canadian ophthalmologist Jean Carruthers was treating her patients in Vancouver with the same drug. Over time, her staff noticed that her patients were looking healthier, more vibrant, and even *younger* every time they came back for a treatment. This amazing phenomenon led Dr. Carruthers and her husband, Dr. Alistair Carruthers (a dermatologist) to begin experimenting even on themselves.

In 1989, Occulinum received broader approval. Then in 1991, Allergan bought the company for $9 million and decided to rename it. Shortly thereafter, the Drs. Carruthers published their study on the effect of treatment of frown lines with Allergan's new drug—you guessed it—*Botox*®.

In 2002, the FDA approved Botox for treatment of frown lines. In 2010, Botox gained approval for the treatment of chronic migraines. There are 5 million doses administered annually in North America, which translate into $1.5 *billion* in sales. Allergan has now applied for patents for around 90 different uses.

Although controversial, Botox epitomizes how an orphan drug once designated for a particular condition might progressively receive approval for several other indications.

While past performance is no certain indication of future results, the Botox story provides a great example of the potential for orphan drugs to become the blockbuster of the future.

In 2011, there was a near-record 35 new drug approvals. Of these, two are theranostics, (personalized drugs approved for use in conjunction with a specific diagnostic test); seven are cancer drugs; 10 are for orphan diseases; and a total of 16 were approved under priority review. The year 2010, in contrast, only saw 21 approvals and the outright rejection of two potential blockbuster weight-loss drugs. Increasing opportunities exist for drug makers to pursue alternative research venues, particularly in the areas of theranostics and orphan drugs.

Looking Ahead

Many pharmaceutical companies have implemented changes in their commercial and R&D process and capabilities. For most, they haven't gone far enough. Sustainable leadership in this market requires a radically different development engine and a radically different commercial model. The key requirement is to build a scientific foundation for highly differentiated and sustainable franchises around selected disease states in other words based on integrated diagnostic and therapeutic capability, extensive product portfolios that address needs over a disease continuum, strategic market insight, and in-depth preclinical and clinical expertise.

While excellent science must be a given, it is not enough by itself. Pharmaceutical companies will also need to master the critical building blocks we outlined throughout the chapter. Those that do will be the leaders in the new health-care marketplace.

Endnotes

1. "Big Pharma: How to Regain Success" by Rita E. Numerof, Michael N. Abrams, and Jack Nightingale, *Scrip Magazine* 156 (2006): 15–17.
2. The Impact of Comparative Effectiveness on the Healthcare Marketplace. Saint Lewis: Numerof & Associates, Inc. 2009.
3. J. P. Garnier, "Rebuilding the R&D Engine in Big Pharma," *Harvard Business Review*, 86, no. 5 (2008): 68ff.
4. "Today's Orphan Drug Could Be Tomorrow's Blockbuster" by Rita E. Numerof, *Medical Progress Today Blog*, November 9, 2011, http://www.medicalprogresstoday.com/2011/11/todays-orphan-drug-could-be-tomorrows-blockbuster.php.

Chapter 8

A New Day Is Dawning for Medical Device and Diagnostics Manufacturers

Getting Products to Market: Change Is in the Wind

The medical device and diagnostics industry isn't as much fun as it used to be. Products are aging and increasingly more difficult to differentiate. Market success has attracted more competitors, many from outside the United States. Changing regulatory requirements in the United States and across the globe have resulted in increasing costs and time to develop new products. What's more, regulatory agencies around the world are requiring postmarket data about the long-term safety and efficacy of products, especially when they are used by broader patient populations in real-world settings.

Concerns about the safety of medical devices took center stage in the United States throughout 2011. Recalls and lawsuits in recent headlines have led to scrutiny from the public, directed both at manufacturers and the Food and Drug Administration (FDA).

Congressional pressure focused on giving the FDA the authority to *require* companies to submit postmarket data as a *condition for continued approval* of moderate-risk medical devices under the fast-track process, and would allow the FDA to rescind approval if this condition is not met. While the FDA *already* had broad authority to require postapproval studies, bills working their way through Congress underscore the growing sentiment that medical device manufacturers and the FDA ought to *increase* activities aimed at ensuring product safety. Even in 2010, the Institutes of Medicine also called for an integrated pre- and postmarket regulatory framework aimed at improving device safety.

Unlike other recommendations in their report—for example, the recommendation to scrap the 510(k) approval process altogether—requirements for more postmarket safety surveillance were considered relatively uncontroversial by the device industry and even the FDA.

The reality is that *much* more will be required of manufacturers to comply with postmarket safety surveillance emerging rules *and* to bring products to market. Increasingly, clinical data will be *required* for 510(K) clearance where historically such data was only needed in support of investigational device exemption (IDE) and pre-market approval of (PMA) submissions.

As regulators enact more stringent requirements for medical device safety, reviewing passively acquired complaints through call centers will no longer be sufficient. Companies will need to adopt a more comprehensive approach to ensuring medical device safety throughout the product lifecycle. This will mean more proactive planning for postmarket safety surveillance based on product characteristics (e.g., product novelty, consequences of product failure, device complexity) identified in early product development. But the real challenge will be bringing products to market going forward.

Over the past several years, the medical device industry has been rocked by product recalls, Department of Justice investigations into improper marketing practices, and incidents that highlight potential conflicts of interest with physicians. Product safety concerns are especially predominant, given FDA reports that from 2005 through 2009 over 3,500 medical devices were recalled for potential safety problems. In the first seven months of 2009, more than 1,000 recall notices were sent out, of which over 100 were designated as *Class 1*, involving a defect serious enough to create a "reasonable probability of adverse health consequences or death." To address concerns about device safety and the medical device approval process, the FDA's Center for Devices and Radiological Health (CDRH) conducted an internal review and commissioned the Institute of Medicine (IOM) to review the 510(k) process in 2011.

Perhaps in anticipation of the IOM's report, the FDA has already taken a number of steps to address concerns related to the 510(k) process. CDRH's plan,[2] released in August 2010, specified 25 specific actions to be taken in order to overhaul the 510(k) process, which include issuing draft guidance and proposed regulations. The FDA's plan leaves the current regulatory framework intact, with substantial revisions and an increased emphasis on the scientific evaluation of medical devices in the hope of avoiding future recalls by approving only innovative, safe products.

The IOM released its independent review in July 2011. The taskforce concluded that the 510(k) process is not a reliable premarket screen of safety and effectiveness and recommended that the FDA would be better served by eliminating the 510(k) process altogether, rather than expending any additional resources attempting to improve it. It recommended replacing the current system with an integrated premarket and postmarket regulatory framework to ensure the safety and effectiveness of future devices.

As the FDA's actions demonstrate, even without the IOM's critical findings and recommendations, device companies must expect additional, significant changes to the 510(k) process and postmarket safety requirements. When viewed in the broader context of healthcare reform, comparative effectiveness research, and other current challenges, changes to the 510(k) process have serious implications for device companies.

While the FDA has rejected the IOM's recommendation to replace the 510(k) process, it apparently anticipated this criticism. Within a month of the release of the IOM's report, the FDA issued a number of guidance documents concerning 510(k) modifications, design of medical device clinical studies, postmarket surveillance studies and requirements, and new methods of monitoring clinical trials.[3]

Implications for the Industry

While it's impossible to eliminate risks associated with medical devices, it is clear that the FDA will require more effort, both premarket and postmarket, from device makers to improve safety. There's clearly tension between getting a safe product to the market quickly versus obtaining additional data to ensure safety, a point we address in more detail in Chapter 9.

Given the FDA's ongoing plans to address the 510(k) process, device companies should expect the FDA to be more demanding in reviewing submissions. In addition, companies will need to expand their view of device development and approval to include planning for postmarket safety requirements. While the FDA rejects the IOM's proposed elimination of the 510(k) process, as a practical matter, there is much less disagreement with the IOM's recommendations to improve postmarket surveillance capabilities. As companies respond to demands for clinical evidence to obtain clearance, they need to plan for increased postmarket safety requirements as well. For purposes of postmarket safety surveillance, companies need to examine whether preclinical, clinical, and product development insights about devices are used sufficiently in developing robust postmarket surveillance strategies.

There are a number of implications beyond postmarket requirements for the industry as well. Companies should expect longer 510(k) reviews, as the FDA focuses on its internal processes, safety, and additional oversight. To a certain extent, however, companies should be able to anticipate issues. If a device is invasive or is based on new technology, heightened scrutiny and/or demands for clinical data should be expected. Companies should recognize, in light of the CDRH and IOM reviews, that if there is something new in a device, it will be more difficult to compare it to a predicate, and it's increasingly likely the FDA will require clinical data. As a result, companies probably should expect higher research and development costs and longer product development cycles.

Commercial Challenges

The commercial front isn't immune; advertising and selling costs are also skyrocketing. But the really bad news is just starting to emerge.

Across the world, payers are clamping down on healthcare costs by saying no to new products, line extensions, and price increases. Reacting to the prospect of exponentially increasing liabilities, payers of all types are demanding hard clinical and health economic data to justify any change with bottom-line impact. We've advised our clients that going forward they should expect that growth will depend on very focused strategies and fairly sophisticated product market segmentation—country-by-country, payer-by-payer, and patient-by-patient decisions to pursue a treatment or not, or to choose a newer, more expensive treatment versus an older, less-expensive one.

In addition, as of January 1, 2013, medical device and diagnostic manufacturers will face a 2.3% excise tax. This tax applied to nonretail hospital and physician supplies as well as leases for devices; eyeglasses, contact lenses, hearing aids, and so on are exempt. There are also greater reporting standards designed to increase transparency around payments to physicians (for each event >\$10 or >\$100 annually) and payments to teaching hospitals.

Fraud and abuse will be the subject of greater focus through new rules regarding compliance program integrity. Penalties have increased for individuals and companies, so the criticality of more robust risk assessments, better accountability, and new approaches to fair market value (FMV) governing relationships with physicians is essential, and market claims will need to have data to support them. Medicare has already begun reducing its payment for imaging, concerned about overutilization and its associated costs.

What's less known by many in the industry is how comparative effectiveness research (CER) will impact these changes. As we outlined in Chapter 4, CER represents a significant shift for the entire industry and promises to radically alter the level of government involvement in the way healthcare products and services are developed, delivered, and paid for. CMS views CER as *the* solution to healthcare cost containment.

The medical device industry may be the sector *most strongly impacted* by the rise of CER as a force in the US healthcare marketplace, and the diagnostics industry may be the one *best positioned* to take advantage of the shift toward a cost-effectiveness orientation. Let's look at how this is likely to play out.

CER: The Threat for Medical Devices

There will be a fundamental restructuring of priorities within large segments of the medical device industry, away from incremental improvements that are mostly of interest to surgeons, and toward improvements that are of interest to payers and delivery stakeholders across the continuum of care.[4]

This will put *significant* pressure on device manufacturers to produce products that require fewer ancillary resources (e.g., fewer surgeon hours, less postoperative recovery). Competition from drugs, other devices, and even noninterventional approaches (e.g., watchful waiting) will increase.

The most important implications for medical device manufacturers are expected to be:

- the end of the "last version plus 5%" business model (began in 2008),
- increased pressure to *rightsize* device functionality (started in earnest in late 2010),
- increased competition with drugs (began in 2010), and
- restricted qualification for devices (began in earnest in 2011 in the United States; United Kingdom began 2007).

Furthermore, enormous challenges will emerge as manufacturers are confronted by healthcare delivery organizations struggling to address their three main threats described in Chapter 5: the development of predictive care paths, improved quality (i.e., outcome) metrics, and population management (think shrinking reimbursement and financial risk).

End of the "Last Version Plus 5%" Business Model

The historic operating model for much of the device industry has been to develop a new, incrementally improved version of a device and seek incrementally increased reimbursement for it. This model has been under pressure in the last several years, exacerbated by the global recession. It's likely to come to a screeching halt within the next few years.

There are two primary reasons for its impending demise. First, it effectively reflected a gentlemen's agreement between payers and device manufacturers—keep pushing the frontiers, and we'll keep paying. Often, the improvements were primarily of interest to surgeons, who were in a position to pressure the other stakeholders to make the improved device available. Many industry insiders believe that these improvements had relatively little incremental value and certainly didn't justify significant increases in reimbursement.

Today there is greater scrutiny of the relative value of the product, and many companies have found their products not fetching the increased reimbursement they expected. This will be more common in the years to come. Hospitals, under increasing cost pressure themselves, are also unlikely to try to keep up in the new technology acquisition race unless there is a clear economic and clinical value argument to be made. And, as specialists leave private practice to become employees of healthcare systems, their incentives are increasingly aligned with healthcare executives. The industry faces continued consolidation pressure as these executives work to standardize on a more limited number of products and manufacturers.

As incremental improvements give way to more substantial ones, companies that rely on 510(k) equivalence for the majority of their products will find themselves needing to enhance their capability to conduct clinical research in support of PMAs. Even those that look to contract with clinical research organizations to oversee this research will still need the capabilities that allow them to adequately oversee and monitor the work.[5]

Second, a system that issues guidelines based on research into the cost effectiveness of a treatment regime is not designed to keep up with the newest innovations in treatment. Incorporating a new product into the guidelines means either considering it equivalent to what already exists (which implies that it can't cost any more than the prior technology if it is to be cost effective) or evaluating the evidence to determine the circumstances under which the new product is more cost effective than the old. This takes time, which increases the delay to be expected between incremental increases in reimbursement.

As the extent to which devices compete with drugs increases, the need to develop devices with potential pharmaceutical competition in mind does too. An immediate assessment of the exposure of specific classes of devices that are heavily weighted in the portfolio to drug competition (which is beyond the scope of this book) should be undertaken immediately.

Increased Pressure to Rightsize Functionality

Ongoing and significant pressure to rightsize the therapeutic value of a product for a particular patient population will emerge. CMS will become increasingly unwilling to pay for *excess functionality*—features that most patients won't use or that are deemed to be beyond what are "necessary." This has two impacts. First, it will create markets for older products, extending their lifecycles in spite of the introduction of more sophisticated versions, as long as the functionality of the older model is sufficient for selected patient segments.

It will also mean that the willingness of CMS to increase reimbursement for the newest product extension will depend heavily on the case for marginal economic and clinical value that can be made for the new model. And while there will still be a place for improved functionality at higher cost, the primary emphasis at first will be on defining segments that can get nearly equivalent benefits from less-expensive products. New product development during this phase is less likely to be focused on questions like "Does a ceramic bearing work better than a metallic one?" than "Will this old design still work if we replace the metal with cheaper injection-molded plastic?"

Pressure to produce products that meet, but do not exceed, functionality needs will require that device companies proactively segment the market based on functional requirements globally and within specific regional markets. Product development itself will take on a new aspect in which cost consciousness is given as much weight as technical capability. This will represent a significant cultural change challenge.

Rightsizing of functionality is likely to be among the first objectives of CER. We expect the demand for more functional, less-expensive devices that began in late 2010 to pick up momentum, growing rapidly in 2012 and beyond.

Increased Competition with Drugs

As the drive to more closely link coverage determinations with demonstrated cost effectiveness gets underway, medical devices will be in more direct competition with drugs. Drug therapies are, in many cases, significantly less expensive than surgical ones, and even if less clinically effective, they may, therefore, be more cost effective. In addition, if CMS, like other payers, can replace costly surgeries with drugs for specific classes of patients on the basis of cost, benefit, or risk, this would be an attractive option for them.

Classes of devices that are especially likely to be subjected to renewed efforts to compare outcomes include: stents and angioplasty devices; implantable stimulation devices for pain relief and Parkinson's disease; and continuous blood glucose monitors and insulin pumps, devices used in bariatric surgery, joint replacements, and spinal surgery.

The expectation that these classes of devices will come under increased scrutiny does not mean that they will necessarily lose out to drug therapies—some may become the new standard of care. Others, however, may find their use restricted to very specific populations. Still others may be demoted behind competitors' products as a second-line treatment on the basis of cost or performance.

Restricted Qualification for Devices

As cost effectiveness becomes a critical factor for determining coverage and reimbursement, certain populations that once were candidates for devices may lose their eligibility. This has happened in the United Kingdom, where, in 2005, the Suffolk Primary Care Trust (part of the National Health Service [NHS]) started to deny orthopedic implants to obese patients and smokers. This practice has spread to include other regions of the country, as well as other procedures (such as in vitro fertilization [IVF]).

Impact of CER on Medical Device Operations

The end of the "last version plus 5%" model will mean a radical change in the way that medical device companies develop products, manage their portfolios, and plan for the future.

In the past, this pricing/reimbursement model has often meant creating features that improve ease of use for surgeons, who would then effectively demand that payers reimburse the product. This model is failing as surgeons begin to accept responsibility for cost containment and as they lose power relative to payers. It has also been impacted by a more active Office of Inspector General/Department of Justice (OIG/DOJ), which is forcing companies to avoid the appearance of a cozy relationship with surgeons. This doesn't mean that surgeon-focused improvements are finished—they'll still have a place—but unless the surgeons themselves are willing to pay for them, they'll have to be of a nature that allows the cost to be passed through to payers, patients, or institutional providers.

For the most part, the incremental model will be replaced, which means that product development will have to refocus on creating *substantial* differentiation between new products and older, competing ones. What's more, this differentiation will have to be along dimensions that matter to payers—CMS's interest in cost effectiveness being a primary example—or that matter to other parties who can supplement reimbursement payments out of their own pockets.

The most obvious examples are premium devices for specific patients who believe that such a device is appropriate for their specific circumstances— for example, the 80-year-old heart patient who can pay extra for a 50-year pacemaker and believes himself likely to take advantage of the extended product life, or the aging athlete who would benefit from a more advanced knee implant than his or her insurance will cover, or the young person who really needs a 60-year knee, or the elderly patient who would benefit from a knee that self-adjusts to help maintain balance.

There are other possibilities, however. Payment doesn't necessarily have to come from the patient—specialty hospitals, hospital systems, and surgical group practices might be willing to cover part of the cost of a device (or of related capital equipment) if doing so allowed them to be perceived as cutting edge, or if some features significantly shortened or simplified surgery or follow-up.

An example of this kind of improvement would be the ability to remotely monitor the performance of a joint implant—a potential up-sell opportunity to both the patient (who may be able to avoid the inconvenience and cost of follow-up visits) and the provider (who may be able to avoid the time and trouble of the visit). In part, the appeal of this kind of improvement depends on how reimbursement works—a return to a capitation-like system (as is currently happening in rehab with bundling of payment for post-acute care services) makes such innovations far more appealing to the providers, while episodic payment for each follow-up visit makes it more appealing to payers. But someone will certainly benefit.

Perhaps the most radical possibility is the development of *better-than-normal* devices—artificial joints, ligaments, and even sensory devices that enhance the capabilities of patients beyond what is natural. These *bionics* (in the 1980s sense of the term) could potentially appeal to younger, healthy patients willing to spend out of pocket to, effectively, upgrade their personal hardware.

The *last version plus* model is already under significant pressure, but the most radical break with the past will come when CMS, in keeping with the actions of its global counterparts, demands evidence of clinical impact and cost effectiveness—in terms of patient-specific outcomes and raw dollars—of a new device as a precondition for reimbursement. This would require a change in the relevant legislation—changes that have been in the works and are likely to be realized in the next couple of years.

Given the potentially catastrophic impact this will have on the value of current product pipelines, it seems prudent to diversify away from this model immediately, as many leading global device manufacturers have begun to do.

Prudent Responses and Defensive Strategies for Medical Device Companies

Over the last several years, we've recommended that medical device companies pursue four key defensive responses:

- Adopt strategies suited to the new environment.
- Focus on reducing the cost of the procedure.
- Develop service wraps.
- Embrace the cost–functionality trade-off.

We stand by these recommendations as the market evolves.

Adopt Strategies Suited to the New Environment

Diversifying away from a business model that emphasizes incremental changes with the surgeon as primary customer to one that identifies and incorporates features that add significant value to payers, patients, and providers should continue to be an immediate concern for device manufacturers.

This requires (1) identifying what constitutes value for these distinct groups of stakeholders and understanding how these values vary within each, (2) refocusing research and Licensing and Acquisition (L&A) efforts on delivering value, and (3) ensuring that evidence generation strategies result in a compelling demonstration of value.

Device companies can also help themselves by taking a step back from a product-focused view of treatment, which tends to keep them locked into a pattern of creating the next version of the last product, in favor of a broader view of the disease state. Intervention after things reach the acute stage will give way, partly, to prevention and early intervention. With the right approach, device makers can be a part of that.

Focus on Reducing the Cost of the Procedure

To the extent that the surgical or procedural costs associated with the use of a device can be reduced by new design, these will make devices more attractive relative to alternatives like drug therapy and no treatment. This should be a specific focus of device makers looking to develop new products.

Develop Service Wraps

To an even greater extent than for pharmaceutical companies, device companies can increase the value of their offerings by bundling them with well-designed services. The development of services that help to ensure that follow-up care goes well or that the additional health benefits made possible by a device (like the cardiovascular benefits that could accrue to a person with a joint replacement if they engaged in regular exercise) could add significant value to payers, providers, or patients. One illustrative example already seeing considerable activity is remote monitoring technology. To the extent that technology can report on the performance of a device and reduce the need for expensive interactions with providers (e.g., follow-up visits), it is likely to be codified into standard protocols for managing care.

Approaches that focus on providing rehabilitation services that are tailored to the needs of the individual may also play a role. By expanding the scope of the business to include things like sports medicine programs or support for those recovering from an injury, or rehabilitation services after surgery, the value proposition can be expanded.

Like pharmaceutical companies, device makers are likely to find that hospital systems and even surgical groups are willing partners in this development work, especially to the extent that developing a new standard of care that offers the wrapped services (a) helps to differentiate them from the competition, and (b) positions them favorably should this treatment protocol be adopted as the standard of care in the eventual guidelines.

Embrace the Cost–Functionality Trade-Off

Rather than always seeking to stay at the forefront of technology, medical device manufacturers should embrace the diversity of needs that exist globally. This means extending the lifecycle of products that might otherwise have been retired to meet more basic needs and limited budgets of population segments across the globe. It means further that payers, providers, and patients globally are moving in the direction of cost–functionality trade-offs.

CER: The Opportunity for Diagnostics

Unlike medical devices, diagnostics are in a great position to take advantage of the shift toward a cost-effectiveness orientation.[6] The ability of diagnostic tests to segment patients based on scientific criteria so that eligibility for various treatments can be restricted and sequenced represents an enormous opportunity. The transition won't be painless, however. The use of diagnostics will become subject to protocol and will need to be justified by demonstrating economic and clinical value.

The most important implications are expected to be reduced tolerance for redundant testing, a new commercial model, and the possibility of mass screening. Each of these is explored in the following sections.

Reduced Tolerance for Redundant Testing

The first impact of CER on the diagnostic industry is likely to be restricted reimbursement for the use of tests to confirm a diagnosis already made on the basis of other tests. This application has been under attack for decades, but physicians— sometimes pressured by patients, sometimes responding to malpractice fears, and sometimes feeling a need for an added measure of certainty—have continued to order them.

This demand won't disappear, but CMS and other payers will increasingly create bureaucratic barriers to the use of multiple tests that target the same diagnosis, and this will rapidly reduce demand. As a result, diagnostics companies are likely to see a reduction in the number of tests performed. The impact will fall most heavily on those tests that purport to measure the same thing—markers of inflammation (e.g., erythrocyte sedimentation rate and C-reactive protein) or imaging techniques. This will force physicians to choose a preferred test, which will be the one they believe to be more diagnostically effective.

Eventually, these individual preferences will give way to specific guidance regarding the tests that are recommended in a particular situation, a decision that will be based on cost effectiveness rather than solely on diagnostic effectiveness.

Initial steps in this direction have already begun and are likely to accelerate as a function of consolidation and reimbursement pressure on delivery organizations. Even the American Medical Association (AMA) has weighed in, attempting to place bounds on the appropriate use of diagnostic imaging.

New Commercial Model

A new commercial model will become prevalent, as the customer changes radically. Currently, the focal customer for the diagnostics sales force is the lab director, with physicians a secondary target. In the future, two new groups will be the primary targets—payers and hospital administrators. As standard (cost-effective) protocols come to dominate medical practice, inclusion of a diagnostic test in the protocol (on the basis of a compelling economic and clinical value argument) will be paramount.

We expect that there will be two sources of protocols in the United States—CMS and hospitals. CMS's interest will be in developing cost-effective ways to treat patients (primarily outpatients) who don't fall under the diagnosis-related group (DRG) system, holding down their costs. This will tend to give license to administrators who want cost-effective guidelines developed and enforced within their hospitals to hold down costs of (primarily inpatient) treatment when there are fixed DRG payments.

This puts diagnostics makers in a position of having to demonstrate that the use of their tests as part of a treatment algorithm leads to more cost-effective treatment. That means significantly more up-front effort to define the value of possible new diagnostic tests from payer and administrator perspectives, select those that have a compelling potential value proposition, and demonstrate the value of the test prior to seeking reimbursement for it. The goal will be to get the new test incorporated into existing or new predictive care paths, as a standard element, as quickly as possible.

If the lab directors and physicians become less important to the sales efforts, there will be a reprioritization of resources away from sales, and toward research and development, clinical trials, and health economics.

Possibility of Mass Screening

It's possible that some diagnostics companies will hit the jackpot if a proprietary test becomes standard (i.e., is incorporated into CMS guidelines) as a widely applicable, even population-wide, preventive screening measure.

In order to make this happen, diagnostics companies will have to focus on developing evidence that the test significantly improves the ability to distinguish people who would benefit from an intervention from those who won't. This may lead to partnerships or agreements with drug or device manufacturers, or with providers that have developed new treatment protocols, because identifying those people who would maximally benefit from their product or service increases their value propositions.

Impact of CER on Diagnostics Manufacturer Operations

The shift to new evidence requirements and a new commercial model will lead to a change in the way that diagnostic tests are developed, because more accurate determination of the probable success of the test in the marketplace will be possible. Hence, more thought and effort will go into determining what test should receive priority in the development process, and more effort will go into defining and conducting trials to support its value proposition.

Diagnostics companies need to begin the shift to a new commercial model immediately. Changes to the diagnostics market space, such that guidelines effectively determine the success of a product, means that an effective economic and clinical value argument will be of paramount importance.

To the extent that guidelines make more distinctions regarding which patients should receive what treatment, testing (particularly genetic and biomarker testing that identifies optimal treatments) could play a much larger, more pivotal role. *This represents a significant opportunity for diagnostics makers.*

Given the lead time involved in product development and approval, those diagnostics companies that begin to put in place the infrastructure to successfully incorporate economic and clinical value into their decision making and to generate data in support of the economic and clinical value of current and next-generation products will be in a powerful position. Those that don't will be in a very weak one.

The potential blockbuster effect of a mass screening hit means that diagnostics companies should begin to take prudent steps toward developing such tests today.

In some cases, relatively inexpensive, primarily retroactive research may allow diagnostics companies to identify candidate drug or device partners (i.e., drug or device makers). The goal of such research would be to identify patients who have responded well to drug A (but not drug B), and to drug B (but not drug A), and apply the diagnostic test to see if it can discriminate between the two groups.

This may require an expansion of the clinical research group (or of the group that oversees clinical trials conducted externally), as well as up-front investment in developing partnerships with drug and device makers. It has the benefit, however, of identifying potential partners whose own products have a great deal to gain from the success of the diagnostic test. Many of these companies have the deep pockets necessary to support the research that will be required to create a compelling economic and clinical value argument for the use of the diagnostic test.

Prudent Responses and Defensive Strategies for Diagnostics

As with device manufacturers, we've made recommendations to our diagnostics clients to pursue two key approaches: diversify the revenue base and begin to develop partnerships for custom diagnostics. We stand by these recommendations and discuss each in the following sections.

Diversify the Revenue Base

As with other segments of the healthcare industry, it will be important for diagnostics companies to look for sources of revenue beyond the formal, reimbursed setting. Many diagnostic tests are already sold over the counter, so this strategy isn't a foreign one. Still, it might be expanded by considering the market of those who "just want to be sure," either through a broader over-the-counter set of offerings or through retail clinics.

As an example of the former, blood glucose monitors might find an expanded niche by appealing to those who don't have diagnosed diabetes, but would like to "make sure," perhaps because they have a family history of diabetes. A low-cost, limited-use test might offer a convenient way for such a person to put his or her mind at ease, while simultaneously reducing the burden on the healthcare system that would result if he or she went the traditional route.

Likewise, a test (or battery of tests) offered through a retail healthcare clinic that allowed a patient to determine his or her risk of developing significant heart disease would be likely to appeal to a reasonably large segment of the population. These clinics are typically staffed by medical professionals, who would be able to lend their clinical judgment to the interpretation of the results.

The point is that cost effectiveness as calculated by a large payer does not account well (if at all) for the value of factors like reduced anxiety or the increased sense of control a person may derive from having a diagnostic test performed. The result is that there will be a large number of people for whom the test would have significant value, but for whom the test will not be covered. Providing access to it in a retail setting has the potential to be very valuable.

Begin to Develop Partnerships for Custom Diagnostics

The development of custom diagnostics in support of personalized medicine presents an enormous opportunity, but it's one in other words best realized if diagnostics makers partner with drug or device makers, or with providers, to demonstrate the combined value of screening in association with the device or therapeutic agent. This will allow diagnostics companies to find partners for the high-powered trials required to convince a skeptical audience of the economic and clinical value of the diagnostic test.

Where a compelling argument can be made that a given diagnostic assay will successfully discriminate between individuals who will—and will not—be helped by a drug, device, or treatment protocol, it makes sense to begin to seek partnerships immediately. Even when there is no *single* diagnostic marker that seems likely to successfully discriminate the treatable from the untreatable, the possibility that a multivariate index assay will make that discrimination possible may be enough to support a partnership.

Where Do Medical Device and Diagnostics Companies Go from Here?

For companies that have relied on fast approval cycles and limited or no clinical data, the future will assuredly be far more demanding. They will be confronted with greater clinical data requirements—and associated expenses—and will need to develop an improved understanding of the clinical value of their products. As the FDA addresses its internal process issues, however, companies may benefit from the development of clearer standards that enable them to gain a better understanding of FDA expectations and requirements, and by extension, they will be able to anticipate hurdles to regulatory approval and plan appropriately.

In the long term, device and diagnostics companies should expect greater importance to be placed on health economics data as well. This will present a number of challenges for these companies. Even as the FDA deals with internal disputes about process, companies must be clear about the path they want to take, work with reviewers to make their case for comparison to a predicate very clear, and know the rules and regulations better than reviewers.

The commercial landscape will see accelerated pricing pressures globally, which will go beyond reduced reimbursement rates. The year 2011 saw increased attention to bundled pricing as organizations try to build on previous work done by centers such as Geisinger and Kaiser. There will also be increased engagement of specialists in employment models and *accountability networks* in the United States continuing to dampen the role of individual surgeons in product decision making.

Focus on patient selection, outcomes, prevention, early diagnosis, and optimal intervention will continue and move the society from a sickness model of healthcare delivery to one of health maintenance and wellness over time. The role of the consumer in healthcare will continue to evolve, with efforts aimed at creating greater accountability. *Consumer Reports*, for example, launched a new division several years ago focused on the evaluation of healthcare delivery organizations and reported on cost, comparing alternative therapies.[7]

We can expect increased pressure for transparency in the United States. The global economic challenges will continue to accelerate cost cutting in the developed world, making the developing world a bigger opportunity *and* source of competitive threat. We expect that demand outside the United States (OUS) for less-complex, less-expensive products requiring support will migrate to the United States and that

OUS competitors will begin to encroach on the United States market, causing technology gaps to close.

The dominant business model of this segment of the healthcare industry, like its counterpart segments, shows signs of entering the *decline* phase of its lifecycle.

The definition of the *customer* has evolved and the relative importance of that customer in decision making will continue to change at an accelerated rate. It's harder and harder to differentiate, pressures toward commoditization are increasing, and market share changes slowly (despite hand-to-hand combat).

As stated earlier, in the United States, as CMS focuses increased attention on outcomes, private insurers are following suit and larger employers will fall in line. There will be increased concern over appropriate diagnosis, and choice of intervention for a given patient will become increasingly important with stringent guidelines (e.g., what drugs, including which cancer regimens, are likely to work for which types of tumors). These groups will also look for comparisons between drugs and classes of drugs (e.g., benefits of generics vs. newer, branded products), and nonsurgical intervention will become more salient as the evidence for operative success continues to be scrutinized (e.g., drugs vs. stents, drugs and physical therapy vs. surgery for lower back pain).

Physician customer loyalty has been a function of sales representative relationships, some product features (although most believe core products are interchangeable), and involvement in clinical studies and product development (which furthers physician identification with the product and profitability). *As a basis for differentiation, this is not sustainable going forward.*

CMS, working closely with the Agency for Healthcare Research and Quality (AHRQ) and the FDA in keeping with other developed markets, will continue to focus on the economic and clinical value of new products (i.e., cost effectiveness). This places the burden on medical device and diagnostics companies to *proactively* evaluate the value of their products (it's not just about *approval*, it's also about reimbursement). Economic and clinical value considerations will have to be an integral part of R&D, business development, and commercial activity. It is imperative that these companies create products of real value to patients, providers, and payers. Economic and clinical value (ECV) considerations must be considered early and will require a redefinition of roles and capabilities. Health economics must be integrated into market strategy. R&D, marketing, and clinical will need to be closely aligned to ensure cost effectiveness and product value *relative to existing treatment.*

Within the current paradigm, most manufacturers have focused on incremental product improvement to the exclusion of game-changing innovation. They've pursued the idea that some improvement is needed to ensure fundamental functionality and product performance and additional features/functionality has been aimed at competitive positioning and delighting major customers. Yet, at some point, performance outstrips real need/value (manufacturers create more functionality than is required or can be legitimately paid for), and the price-to-value ratio begins to shrink and the stage is set for commoditization. The medical device and diagnostics industry is at a critical point where it is vulnerable to game-changing technology (and market disruption) that redefines price-to-value expectations. Questions manufacturers should be asking themselves include:

- Does *x* really work?
- How much product performance are my stakeholders willing to pay for?
- How much representative support am I willing to pay for?
- How important (valuable) are the clinical outcomes we can demonstrate?
- What real economic and clinical value do branded products provide over older technology?

Savvy medical device and diagnostics marketers have built their reputations and success focused on the surgeon-as-customer. Sales strategy and process have been defined on the premise that the surgeon was the only decision maker that counts, because they define patient needs, and that drives clinical choices. This has been a relatively simple sale, managed through a rep organization focused on building relationships with surgeons and providing them with the surgical liaison services they've come to expect.

Manufacturers and surgeons are now caught up in a reform environment focused on better health outcomes at lower cost. As argued throughout the book, this objective is putting tremendous pressure on *all* stakeholders—payers, providers, and manufacturers—to rethink their business models and challenge fundamental assumptions about their customers, their products and services, their prices, and how they go to market.

Amid this tumult, a new competitive landscape is rapidly emerging. The once-straightforward device and diagnostics purchase decision must now satisfy hospital administrators faced with declining reimbursement, as well as surgeons. Building organizational capability to identify and meet the institutional needs of the hospital-as-customer is now a prerequisite for continued market success.

Hospital-as-Customer Requires a New Sales Model

The hospital–manufacturer relationship needs to be moved from a winner/loser price negotiation to a win/win/win partnership among hospital, surgeon, and manufacturer. The basis for this partnership is the shared interest in efficiency, margin, patient satisfaction, surgeon satisfaction, quality, and safety. The range of ways in which manufacturers can impact these objectives needs to be explored and explicitly understood.

This requires an executive-to-executive relationship. The manufacturer's representative must have the business acumen to surface nonobvious needs beyond the product itself and the ability to translate those opportunities into concrete action plans for the manufacturer and the hospital.

With their focus on surgeon customers, traditional device and diagnostics reps haven't built strong relationships with hospital executives, and they are often not well positioned to do so. They lack credibility to explore strategic business issues because they are seen as transactional salespeople trying to preserve price. Institutional value requires a dialogue that should be outside the context of contract negotiations, and focused on how the collective capability of the manufacturer can enhance service line growth, profitability, and outcomes.

Developing a capable hospital relationship management resource is just one part of the necessary new commercial model. Hospital-as-customer also implies more precise hospital targeting criteria by the manufacturer, focusing its value-creating relationship management resources on those hospitals most able to appreciate total value versus device cost.

Many hospitals aren't yet sophisticated enough to be looking for a total value proposition from a manufacturer relationship, but they're getting there. This can be accelerated by taking the lead in helping them recognize what they should be asking for.

The new winners in this market will be the first to establish and manage hospital executive relationships that collaboratively identify and implement a new business model and approach to care that delivers better outcomes at a lower cost.

Endnotes

1. "Marketing a New Process" by Stephen E. Rothenberg and Jill E. Sackman, *MX: Medtech Executive*, December 2011.

2. US Food and Drug Administration, "CDRH Plan of Action for 510(k) and Science: Implementation of Recommendations from the 510(k) and Science Reports," http://www.fda.gov/AboutFDA/CentersOffices/OfficeofMedicalProductsandTobacco/CDRH/CDRHReports/ucm239448.htm.

3. US Food and Drug Administration documents: Draft Guidance for Industry and FDA Staff, *510(k) Device Modifications: Deciding When to Submit a 510(k) for a Change to an Existing Device* (July 27, 2011); Draft Guidance for Industry, Clinical Investigators, and Food and Drug Administration Staff, *Design Considerations for Pivotal Clinical Investigations for Medical Devices* (August 15, 2011); Draft Guidance for Industry and Food and Drug Administration Staff, *Factors to Consider When Making Benefit-Risk Determinations in Medical Device Premarket Review* (August 15, 2011); Draft Guidance for Industry and Food and Drug Administration Staff, *Procedures for Handling Section 522 Postmarket Surveillance Studies* (August 16, 2011); Guidance for Industry, *Oversight of Clinical Investigations—A Risk-Based Approach* (August 2011).

4. *The Impact of Comparative Effectiveness on the Healthcare Marketplace* (Saint Louis: Numerof & Associates, Inc., 2009).

5. The FDA is in the process of moving to a more stringent definition of what qualifies for 510(k) approval, independent of these considerations.

6. Numerof & Associates, *Impact of Comparative Effectiveness*.

7. "Joint Replacement: 1001 Patients Tell You What Your Doctor Can't," *Consumer Reports*, June 1, 2006.

Chapter 9

Putting Value at the Center of Healthcare

Over the last several years, there's been a fever-pitched drumbeat to *do healthcare reform* and to do it *now*. This culminated in 2010 with passage of landmark legislation whose 2,700 pages purported to "fix the system." Regardless of the Supreme Court's decision on the constitutionality of the individual mandate and severability, the healthcare industry needs reform, and policy makers have an important role in enabling that to happen.

While we agree that *healthcare reform* is an incredibly important topic and needs to be addressed, it means many different things to different people—it's complex, the problem didn't just emerge, and we need to be mindful of what exactly we're reforming. There are always unintended consequences to any action, no matter how well intended. Once in place, it is very difficult to dismantle legislation and the bureaucracy put in place to realize it. The primary rule of medicine is probably worth remembering—*first, do no harm*.

In short, healthcare reform wasn't well enough defined to act on despite the vote on March 23, 2010. And it was clearly an attack on the insurance sector. As we noted in Chapter 2, healthcare is big business, and every component has an agenda to pursue and a stake in the outcome. All need to change. What it means in many quarters is understood only in relatively vague terms: for example, affordable insurance, better outcomes for our dollar, and higher quality at lower costs. In our experience, organizations that lack precision in what they're trying to do always fail.

While it's generally recognized that there are three parts to any type of serious healthcare reform—insurance coverage, delivery, and payment—recent legislation really only addresses the first part and did so at great cost and complexity.

Access has frequently been cited as another issue that healthcare reform needed to address. The population that doesn't have access is often poorly defined, and there are many examples of clinics that offer free care that aren't used— appointments aren't kept, sometimes aren't even made, and the general issues of health habits and adherence that plague mainstream society crop up here, too.

Without a clear, coherent (and relatively simple) strategy defining the underlying issues that we're solving for, piecemeal solutions will only aggravate the problems that we have today. We have already spent resources we can't afford, and we risk spending more without correcting the inefficiencies in the system as it is structured today. We need to be sure that people understand how we got to the situation we have (which clearly isn't working), what keeps the current system in place, and the myriad options that could help to resolve gaps.

Once we have this "diagnosis," and we understand how the component parts reinforce a status quo that most would agree isn't optimal, we can define a set of principles to guide innovations to improve the situation. These can be implemented in a "reasonable" time period with interventions that are staged, sustainable, effectively coordinated, and achieve a simple goal—improved patient outcomes at reduced cost.

One could argue that once we deal with insurance sector–specific problems related to coverage restrictions for preexisting conditions, continuity, transparency, choice, and service, healthcare delivery is at the heart of real reform. All the other sectors we've discussed in earlier chapters feed into healthcare delivery—selling products and services directly or indirectly to consumers who engage with providers and delivery organizations to attempt to get better health outcomes at lower cost. Because reform of healthcare delivery is so central in this equation, it is a major focus of this chapter. While the legislation put in place a framework to begin experiments to address changes in delivery and payment through subsequent and complex administrative rule writing, these efforts have been wholly inadequate.

Recent Legislative Solutions and Why They Won't Work

As we discussed earlier in this book, the Patient Protection and Affordable Care Act (PPACA) is the most recent effort to address the problems of the healthcare system. The legislation attempted to address the high and unsustainable costs of the system and provide greater access to care for the uninsured. Yet, while these goals are noble, the solution PPACA offered is fundamentally flawed. The requirements outlined in PPACA would create administrative behemoths that will limit individual choice, increase bureaucracy, and ultimately drive up costs!

Two of the central, and ironically most onerous, provisions enacted by PPACA are accountable care organizations (ACOs) and state insurance exchanges. The intent of these efforts was well meaning, but the resulting regulations would serve to increase bureaucracy, fragmentation, and costs without improving outcomes. Let's discuss these in more detail.

Accountability for Care Is a Good Concept

ACOs: Their Original Purpose

Accountability for care is not a new concept.[1] It entered the spotlight in the 1990s through such programs as *pay-for-performance* and various managed care initiatives that were intended to create "greater accountability on the part of providers for their performance."[2] In this context, the locus for accountability was limited to individual providers and did not address the need for integrated delivery of quality care.[3] In order to address the need for provider accountability across an integrated care continuum, a new model, the accountable care organization, was proposed. The ACO model developed as a way of addressing accountability of both healthcare providers and the delivery systems in which they practice, collaborate, and interact.[4]

ACOs are offered as a solution to the "serious gaps in quality and widespread waste" within the healthcare system.[5] The underlying intent of the ACO model was to address the lack of financial incentives for reducing costs while improving quality, coordination, and consistency of care.[6]

Evolving concept: The ACO concept has evolved since its inception several years ago. Most proponents of ACOs agree that they should, at a minimum, offer services across the continuum of care and in various institutional settings; be able to budget and forecast resource needs; and be *large enough* to sustain reliable and universal performance measurements.[7] By working with local providers already centered around and connected to one or more hospitals, it's presumed that physicians and hospitals can create an "organized system" that payers could then hold accountable for improvements in quality of care and costs.[8]

At the conceptual level, the incentive for ACOs would be to increase efficiency and avoid overuse and duplication of services, resources, and facilities. In this model, ACO members would share in the savings resulting from the increased coordination of care.

Nowhere in these discussions was there an attempt to enable a simplified market-based solution that puts patients at the center, requires transparency of cost and outcomes, and ensures that primary care physicians would play the critical role of healthcare quarterback on behalf of their patients.

ACOs: Their Role in PPACA

PPACA mandates a shared savings program among healthcare providers, which generally follows the ACO model discussed above, but does not include provisions to test real-world feasibility in a controlled way. In effect, the legislation is an experiment with unknown consequences. Through this program, ACOs are awarded their portion of the shared savings if they sufficiently reduce costs and simultaneously improve quality. The ACOs themselves will be tasked with distributing savings among participating providers, who will likely continue to be reimbursed on a fee-for-service basis. Aside from retaining the current fee-for-service reimbursement system, PPACA does not indicate how savings should be divided among participants.[9] This situation creates a moral hazard, as providers will be incented to do less for patients, perhaps waiting before authorizing needed tests or withholding treatments longer than might be optimal. They would essentially be replaying the experience of health maintenance organizations (HMOs) in the 1980s, a topic covered in the next section.

PPACA describes ACOs as provider groups that accept responsibility for the cost and quality of care delivered to a specific population of patients cared for by the groups' participating clinicians. The legislative intent is that these groups will have an incentive to invest in infrastructure and redesigned care for high-quality and efficient delivery of services. From an organizational standpoint, however, PPACA defines ACOs only loosely, and eligibility requirements are vague.

An ACO may include different participating groups, such as physician groups and hospitals, which are to coordinate their services. Eligible organizations must have a formal legal structure, must include enough primary care providers for 5,000 Medicare fee-for-service beneficiaries, and must contract or employ any additional providers that their patient population requires. They must be prepared not only to meet specified performance standards, but also to measure and report quality outcomes in a uniform manner as required by the Centers for Medicare and Medicaid Services (CMS), using highly integrated information systems.[10]

While steps to improve quality performance by standardizing metrics and reporting requirements are mandated in PPACA, requirements in the legislation are largely ambiguous, as performance standards and metrics are still undefined. The specifics will be determined by the Department of Health and Human Services (HHS) and will include areas such as clinical processes and care, patient experience, and the amounts and rates of services rendered.

As developed in PPACA, ACOs would create what are, in effect, *virtual organizations* composed of local hospitals and affiliated providers covering groups of patients.[11] There are no enrollment requirements for patients, who will be assigned to ACOs based on which provider they visit most frequently and may not even be aware of the ACO's existence. The performance standards that ACOs will be expected to meet will use metrics data collected from uniform information systems, which the ACOs themselves are required to implement. ACO spending will be measured against a comparable target (historic data for the same or similar patient population). If an ACO meets its performance and quality standards (which remain largely undefined), the ACO will share in any savings.[12]

Government-Sponsored Payment and Delivery Systems

Given the enormous size of the Medicare program, Medicare policy changes have a profound influence on private-sector health insurance practices, including payment systems.[13] Congressional leaders have long attempted to improve quality and lower costs by developing complex payment and delivery systems intended to increase accountability.

In the 1980s, Congress created a prospective payment system (PPS) for Medicare in an effort to control rising healthcare costs in hospitals.[14] Under this new system, hospitals were reimbursed a predetermined amount for each diagnosis-related group (DRG) (category of inpatient cases).

This new strategy was intended to place pressure on organizations to increase efficiency and minimize unnecessary spending, as they would only be reimbursed a set amount for each diagnostic category. To give organizations a way of monitoring provider efficiency by DRG category, resource-based relative-value units (RBRVUs) were introduced. RBRVUs, however, continued to reimburse providers on a fee-for-service basis and reflected a highly complex set of calculations.[15]

Since they are paid for each service they provide, not for the outcomes they help patients achieve, providers continued to have a profit-based motive not to ensure the quality and efficiency of patient care, but to increase volume at the service code level. As a result, these changes did not ultimately translate to lower spending. In fact, they resulted in more spending, reduced the quality of care, empowered specialists to deliver more nonintegrated and perhaps unnecessary care, and diminished the core role of primary care providers as "quarterbacks" or "gatekeepers" responsible for managing, coordinating, and directing patient care in the most efficient way possible. Fee-for-service, activity-based provider payment creates no incentive for providers to increase efficiency and acts as a disincentives for those who take more time to coordinate care, because they don't get paid for time not spent with the patient.

With the Health Maintenance Organization Act of 1973, Congress directly promoted the growth of managed care arrangements in the private sector. In the 1990s, private organizations and employers sponsored HMOs, PPOs, and physician-hospital organizations (PHOs) as part of their managed care efforts to reduce costs by eliminating provider incentives for inappropriate care and excess productivity.[16]

These *managed care organizations* would often enter into capitated arrangements with contracted providers, where these providers would receive a fixed amount per patient member of the organization that chose to seek care through that provider. Capitated payments were determined based on historic fee-for-service (FFS) data. These efforts were intended to emphasize primary care as central to improving healthcare and keeping hospital costs under the capitated amount.

Yet capitation created a new profit motive that was equally, if not more, detrimental to patients than productivity incentives created by FFS plans. Because payment was not tied to outcomes, capitation encouraged providers to cut spending *without* sufficient concern for patient welfare.[17] We anticipate a similar scenario unfolding with ACOs as attempts to define outcomes connected to payment have been watered down under industry pressure.

Top-Down Approach to Complex Health Policy Problems

Past healthcare initiatives that have relied on organizational structure to address the complex challenge of delivering higher quality at lower cost have not succeeded in improving either efficiency or performance. In fact, they have largely exacerbated the problems they were intended to address. Neither DRGs nor HMOs created a shared goal for all parties.

In both cases, provider profit motives lacked the pressure of consumer demand to preserve quality while minimizing cost. While DRGs and RBRVUs encouraged providers to focus on production without consequences for unnecessary interventions, HMOs and other managed care organizations encouraged providers to minimize intervention, regardless of whether doing so could hinder the quality or completeness of patient care. Outside the HMO model, providers had the perverse incentive to fix the quality problems they frequently created.

In most industries, consumer demand drives service providers and product manufacturers to improve quality while maximizing efficiency. In healthcare, patients are not direct consumers when they don't pay for their care directly. So, providers don't face pressure from the *consumer* to provide high-quality and affordable care. Generally, patients seek care from providers and organizations that are covered under their insurance plan, which, quite often, is selected by their employers. Providers and healthcare organizations negotiate the most favorable rates with payers to protect their revenue stream, without an incentive to increase efficiency or improve quality.

Past attempts at manipulating organizational structure to reduce cost (and implicitly improve outcomes) ignore the underlying problem—the minimal role that consumer (patient) demand plays in driving market competition among providers and organizations. Instead, these efforts have decreased accountability for, and quality of, care by:

■ preserving fee-for-service provider reimbursement, which encourages volume-driven production, not outcomes;
■ favoring large players who consolidate or monopolize the market, thereby reducing competition;
■ reducing the role of primary care providers, who were intended to be gatekeepers of patient care;
■ failing to create accountability that extends across a continuum of care; and

■ failing to require transparency of cost and quality outcomes in order for consumers to make informed choices and create effective competition in the market.

ACOs: Key Deficiencies

As noted, ACOs were introduced to remedy the inadequate accountability for excess spending and quality of patient care. Under PPACA, however, ACOs will likely fail to ensure accountability. Specifically, PPACA provisions have the following:

1. PPACA does not empower consumers to be stakeholders in their own care. The PPACA provisions are obviously not a market-based set of solutions—they do not allow consumers to make fully informed choices about their coverage and care.

Consumer-driven markets do not need to create artificial incentives to improve quality and performance because competitors are constantly working to improve their products, attract consumers, and ultimately increase market share. Except for unique services—cosmetic dermatology and Lasik eye surgery, for instance—the healthcare market does not operate this way. Since employers contract with insurers who enter into arrangements with providers, competition is limited, and the *real* consumer—the patient—has no part in driving that competition. The result has been a lack of transparency and a lack of incentives for healthcare providers to offer quality "products."

Instead of remedying this problem and increasing competition among payers and providers by treating patients as informed consumers, PPACA includes vague requirements for performance measurement and fails to address underlying issues driving cost.

Ironically, many physicians are reluctant to assume accountability for patient outcomes since they recognize that much of the outcome is directly under the behavioral control (and thus accountability) of the patient-consumer. Taking the patient-consumer out of the equation undermines any attempt at creating true accountability for healthcare decisions.

2. PPACA does not encourage provider accountability. Though it seems that provider buy-in would be integral to an ACO's success in the shared savings program, providers continue to be paid for each service they perform. Given the uncertainties and practical complications of distributing savings, the fundamental incentive to provide a service and receive a fee remains in place.

Even with the possibility of a bonus from shared savings, maintaining the fee-for-service system encourages providers to continue delivering an excess of services so that they can maximize their return. By creating incentives for each provider to increase his own productivity, fee-for-service payment undermines the importance of provider collaboration across the continuum of care. Providers have an incentive to *intervene* and *do something* as opposed to engaging in thoughtful discourse and collaboration with patients. Faced with the choice between generating a fee for themselves now or sharing some future possible savings with the entire set of providers, many will opt for the former course of action.

3. PPACA creates an unfair competitive advantage for large organizations. The mandated program centers on a single, untested, and vague model in other words largely hospital-centric. Eligibility requirements, while vague and ambiguous, collectively suggest that larger, more complex organizations have an implicit advantage. Groups of independent practitioners as well as other types of small and mid-sized practices may lack the infrastructure, technology, or other resources needed to qualify and succeed on their own. Also, smaller, entrepreneurial organizations that want to venture alone may find themselves competing against similar physician practices that have joined ACOs or been acquired by larger organizations and, as a result, will be under less financial and clinical pressure to improve efficiency and quality.

Large delivery systems are, once again, able to claim or consolidate their hold on substantial portions of their markets, resulting in less competition. Large systems may become "too big to fail" and will have increased leverage with payers. Without effective competition, they might have little incentive to reduce spending or improve quality of care. Ironically, the most significant costs relate to end-of-life care, hospital inefficiency, and hospitals' inability to manage *never events* (events that should never happen, but do, such as surgery on the wrong limb or transfusion of the wrong blood type). Why reward the very institutions that failed to lead the industry in transformation?

Recommendations for Policymakers: Healthcare Delivery

Throughout this book we've tried to provide some illustrations in a number of key areas to demonstrate concretely why we believe that there is enough money in the system to address issues of access, broader coverage, and so on. Our contention is that business models need to change and it is unlikely that they will unless there is some outside intervention—again, focused on specific principles. Industries and specific organizations, like individuals, frequently don't change until and unless forced to do so. We need to be careful about what we ask them to do or we risk crippling the economy and what has been universally recognized as the best care in the world. We do need to get costs under control and have hard conversations about what we're willing to pay for.

We need a market-based model that would encourage accountability in the healthcare delivery system and stimulate change across the industry, as opposed to relying on an institution to funnel accountability down to the various types of providers. Such a new organizational model for enterprising companies could:

1. *Require accountability from primary care providers and patients for prevention, health maintenance, health education, and primary care.* Primary care providers and patients are the foundation for this model, driving accountability across all four tiers. Primary care providers will be responsible for educating the patient and facilitating prevention, health maintenance, health education, and primary care. They will also be responsible for resuming their traditional role as gatekeepers of patient care by collaborating with providers in other tiers, ensuring mutual accountability, and emphasizing prevention and primary care.

2. *Require accountability from specialists focused on the care continuum, cost efficiency, and increased quality of needed services.* Specialists who demonstrate a commitment to management of care across the care continuum, an emphasis on primary care and prevention, cost efficiency, and increased quality of *needed* services will comprise the second tier of this model. Under this new system, specialists will not be rewarded for the number of services they deliver, but for their contribution to effective, efficient, and tightly integrated delivery of quality care. This requires interdisciplinary communication, collaboration, and a commitment to each patient's best interests.

3. *Require institutional accountability, focused on delivering better outcomes at lower cost, coordinated by primary care physicians.* Hospitals and specialty care organizations will serve as the third tier in this model and will focus on delivering better outcomes at lower costs. They will be responsible for monitoring and managing progress by setting goals, assessing individual performance, and creating internal initiatives to promote collaboration and good practices. Rather than trying to force accountability among

providers, organizations will simply serve as vehicles for integrating providers that have already demonstrated accountability. Again, primary care providers will be integral to coordinating and facilitating these organizational changes.

4. *Promote coordination across community agencies, reinforcing prevention, health maintenance, and disease management.* Responsibility for health and healthcare should not be confined to hospitals and physician practices. In order to truly empower consumers as stakeholders in their own health, concepts like prevention, health maintenance, and disease management should be reinforced at the community level. Private-sector success will spill over into the public sector, and policymakers will be encouraged to hold social service agencies, nursing homes, home health organizations, and other community agencies accountable for continued patient education, support, and advocacy. Public and private entrepreneurs can begin to ensure that prevention, awareness, and accountability become part of a lifestyle that consumers embrace and the healthcare industry is required to sustain.

In theory, ACOs provide financial incentives to organizations that, by encouraging providers to work under a common organizational umbrella, can reduce costs and improve outcomes. In reality, given the complexity of the existing system, such a strategy will not only fail—it will most likely exacerbate the very problems it was designed to fix. ACOs will concentrate more and more power in fewer and fewer organizations, allowing them to become too large to fail. Such a system will undermine competition and entrepreneurship, the bedrock of innovation and job growth in this country. Thus, PPACA creates the potential for increased bureaucracy, fragmentation, and costs without improving outcomes.

There is no evidence that supports the use of untested, complex organizational structures to improve quality of care and reduce costs. Indeed, the evidence suggests the opposite. Only by systematically changing the underlying payment model, enabling competition, and introducing transparency in cost and outcomes will the goals of healthcare reform be achieved. Creating incentives that focus on achieving quality outcomes, providing choice, and allowing real competition are what will transform healthcare delivery to a system that provides higher quality healthcare at lower costs.

In the midst of reform debates, the subject of tort reform is often the focus. The argument goes as follows. Physicians, out of fear of legal action, frequently order more tests and prescribe more drugs than they themselves would argue are medically necessary. One rationale is that patients are pressuring them to do the "latest" just to be sure that the diagnosis is accurate. Since most patients aren't paying anyway, the issue of cost doesn't often come up. So, after the patient rejects an initial suggestion by the doctor that the test isn't really needed, most physicians go ahead and order the test. In the absence of guidelines, physicians are in the awkward position of arguing with the patient.

Under pressure of time, the path of least resistance—ordering the test—seems rational. Until there are more specific guidelines and care paths defining what is optimal for a given condition, this situation is unlikely to change. Indeed, physicians who follow clinical guidelines could be given safe harbor in the event of a subsequent lawsuit.

Enabling Markets to Create Access to Care

As we described in the prior section on ACOs, the same bureaucratic approach characterizes another core element of PPACA, state-based health insurance exchanges. One element of the insurance piece of the puzzle is determining how to expand the number of people who have affordable healthcare coverage. The answer offered by PPACA is to mandate that the uninsured and everyone else purchase coverage, choosing either an employer-offered program, if available, or from a limited range of subsidized and heavily regulated health plans offered via healthcare insurance exchanges that must be created, managed, and funded by each state!

Although the goal of extending healthcare coverage to more of the population is a noble one, the solution PPACA offers is fundamentally flawed and unsustainable. The requirements outlined in PPACA will result in the creation of administrative giants that will limit individual choice and drive up costs. Regardless of challenges to PPACA states have an opportunity to define how they will address their specific needs. States that adopt a market-based approach and encourage the formation of private-sector healthcare insurance marketplaces have the opportunity to address all three parts of reform and achieve the overall objective in the process.

A market-based approach would accomplish the goal of making coverage more affordable and more widely held, but would preserve flexibility for states, preserve choice for consumers and insurers, and avoid the creation of another expensive bureaucracy. A market-based approach is more likely to lead to better health outcomes at lower cost.

Creating Access to Affordable Health Coverage

Most everyone can agree that the high cost of healthcare in the United States is a barrier to access—who among us could afford to pay *full list price* for every drug, office visit, or procedure? Most everyone can also agree that expanding access to care, assuming fundamental changes are made in payment and delivery, would not only be a moral good for society, but would lower healthcare costs over the long term. With greater access to care, individuals would be more likely to seek treatment earlier, when it is generally cheaper to be treated, and would be less likely to wait until they experience an emergency. Likewise, with greater access to care, individuals would also have greater access to prevention and wellness programs, and education about health behaviors that could positively influence health outcomes.[18]

There is general agreement that coverage through a health plan increases access to care, and that coverage options have become unattractive due to their high cost, complexity, and other limitations. Those with mid to high incomes generally enroll in employer-sponsored health plans, where available, which pool risk and share costs in order to gain access to care. Coverage through taxpayer-funded assistance programs (e.g., Medicaid, Medicare) also increases access to care for those with low incomes and for those over 65.[19] Those who don't qualify for assistance programs, or who don't have health plan coverage through their employers, have been forced to do without, hope for the best, wait until they have a health emergency, or elect to purchase coverage on their own.

What everyone doesn't agree on is the best way to increase coverage, or more specifically, enrollment in health plans and assistance programs. PPACA's solution is to combine a personal mandate with state-run exchanges, forcing consumers to choose from a limited slate of commoditized health plans, funded in large part by federal subsidies.

PPACA's solution will limit choice, create new bureaucracies, and cost more, putting additional burdens on the states. There is an alternative—states can create market-based solutions that leverage the laws of supply and demand to enable greater access to more affordable health coverage options.

Recommendations for Policymakers: Access to Care

As we've discussed, health insurance exchanges will accelerate healthcare spending, but ironically, not on healthcare services aimed at improving health. Instead, they will create more bureaucracy and place more burdens on states already strapped for cash. States should take this unique opportunity to focus on their own insurance markets to find out why they don't operate as effectively and efficiently as they should.

Like anything else, state insurance markets evolve over time and are sometimes loaded down with last decade's concerns, or with provisions that just aren't effective, so it's important to review market performance and give the regulatory environment a thorough scrubbing, keeping what works, and discarding what doesn't. State governments shouldn't have to spend a penny more on market regulation, but should rightsize and align regulations so the market can accomplish the desired outcomes of greater access to care by providing more affordable insurance coverage options.

What is the legitimate role for state governments in enabling more efficient markets? Generally, states should look to accomplish the following goals.

1. Ensure legitimacy of participating businesses. States have a clear role to play in registering businesses and making sure market participants are following the rules. For insurers specifically, appropriate consideration must be given to preventing use of inadequate health plan documentation and misleading marketing materials, as well as managing risk so insurers will maintain sufficient financial assets to cover health plan obligations. Healthcare coverage is so complex that insurers can take advantage of consumers through use of industry jargon, medical terminology, or claims about financial strength.

2. Aggressively prosecute fraudulent, negligent, and abusive business practices. For markets to function efficiently, a neutral party like a state regulatory agency can hold market participants accountable to standards of good business practices. Regulators go too far, however, when they try to protect consumers from themselves, attempting to prevent consumers from making unwise or risky choices. Consumers should be free to purchase more or less coverage than the government thinks they need and take responsibility for their decisions.

Some states may need to play a greater role in monitoring and censuring unfair business practices such as denial of claims to stretch out cash flows, changing policies without telling members, or unfairly weeding out sicker members.

3. Remove legislative barriers to competition and consumer choice. In highly efficient markets, sellers compete to develop products that consumers demand. How efficient is the local insurance market at matching consumers with affordable health coverage? A review of local markets will likely reveal significant gaps, some of which are due to specific regulations that could be loosened or removed.

One common barrier to competition is the proliferation of coverage mandates, requirements that all plans offer coverage for a specific disease or treatment. The number of coverage mandates has risen from nearly 1,000 in 1997 to over 2,100 in 2010.[20] Coverage mandates put the government in the role of second-guessing consumers, and each mandate adds cost to all plans for all subscribers when some may not need or want that particular coverage.

Estimates suggest the cumulative effect of coverage mandates adds 20–30% to the cost of premiums.[21] In other words, basic health coverage would be 20–30% cheaper without expensive mandates. States can relax legislative demands on coverage and rely on consumer demand and competition instead: insurers that won't offer the "right" types of coverage will lose market share to those that will, but only if markets operate more efficiently.

Closely related to this idea is the need to enable personalization of health plans. States should remove any barriers to offering a basic catastrophic coverage plan with a menu of additional coverage options.[22] This may require some changes to regulations regarding risk pools so insurers have more flexibility to spread the cost of unusual coverage needs over a wider population of members to keep coverage costs down.

Barriers to competition often exist in the types of organizations that are allowed to offer self-funded plans. Legislators might ask, "Can chambers of commerce or affinity groups form risk pools for self-insured coverage plans?" If not, why not? In Missouri, the Regional Chamber and Growth Association (RCGA) formed a trust 30 years ago so employers could join together to create a larger entity with greater bargaining power, enabling small and mid-sized employers to have group coverage options that would typically be available only to large employers.[23]

4. *Promote transparency so consumers know what they're getting.* For healthcare insurance markets to function more efficiently, consumers need greater transparency about what they are trying to purchase. Legislators should find out what's preventing consumers from making more detailed cost comparisons for health plans.

Currently, it is difficult for consumers to compare available health plans and the insurance companies that offer them. Ideally, consumers would have easy access to useful and relevant data so they could determine which insurers have, for example, the highest member satisfaction, the lowest frequency of serious complaints, the fastest and most accurate claims processing, or the highest medical loss ratios (MLRs). Regulators in some states may need to require expanded public disclosure of essential data so private-sector firms can offer it to the public in a timely and convenient manner.

Similarly, consumers need better tools to understand the mechanics of health plans, especially how health status and lifestyle choices impact premiums. Consumers should be able to answer simple questions like, "How much would I save if I lost 20 pounds?" or "Which plan offers the best discounts to diabetics like me who comply with health management programs?" The data exists: eHealth, Inc. recently published data that shows that, on average, smokers pay 14% more than nonsmokers, and "obese" individuals pay 22.6% more.[25]

You'll recall in Chapter 1 we noted that in every other industry, advancing technology has generally resulted in lower costs and improved products and services. Until we create a true market-based approach to the healthcare industry, we won't be able to crack rising costs and improved outcomes in any meaningful way. Transparency, increased accountability, and competition are the core components of a market-based model for healthcare and will be necessary to achieve the goal of better health outcomes at lower cost.

Supporting Innovation: Finding the Right Balance at the Food and Drug Administration

We've spent the bulk of this chapter with a focus on PPACA and its implications for policy makers going forward in their efforts to support market-based solutions for healthcare delivery. Most of our discussion centered on two major elements of the legislation—ACOs and state-based insurance exchanges. In Chapter 4 we talked about the role of comparative effectiveness research (CER) and how it translates to healthcare delivery and the manufacturers who sell critical products into the sector to support positive health outcomes, namely pharmaceutical, medical device, and diagnostics companies.

We would be remiss if we did not spend at least some focused discussion on the role of the Food and Drug Administration (FDA) as it is the gatekeeper for new products coming into the market, and increasingly, for products staying in the market. Despite intense controversy surrounding the agency—with critics lambasting it for either too little or too much oversight, processes that remain opaque or contradictory, decisions that are made too fast or too slowly—the FDA is in an extraordinarily difficult position, compounded with problems of staffing and staff capability in light of complex, emerging technology and combination products (i.e., drug–device products). Keeping current in this milieu is extraordinarily challenging and raises important questions about the structure and role of the agency—questions that are beyond the scope of this book.

No agency or organization is without flaws and neither is the FDA. The agency regulates the products coming to and staying in the US market. It does so through formal guidance that typically follows a scientific method and requires evidence of the safety and efficacy of the products it reviews. As we noted in Chapter 4, the mandate of the agency is in transition. It has begun to openly engage in discussions around cost with CMS, and we expect cost considerations to be taken into account in reviewing product evidence going forward. Thus, issues concerning the relative "value" of a given product will be considered as part of the regulatory approval process (e.g., does Product X, which costs more than Y, deliver superior outcomes to warrant bringing it to market? Does Product A, which is similar to B but costs much less, provide market value warranting its approval?)

In a nutshell, this dynamic is at the heart of discussions concerning accelerated approval for biosimilars and generics on the pharmaceutical side, as well as 510(k) devices. Pressure has mounted against the approval of "me-too" products, and there is more scrutiny regarding the rigor of evidence being brought forward—not just for reimbursement, but for regulatory approval as well.

These dynamics are very important as we think about the underlying objective of healthcare reform—better outcomes at lower cost. And the FDA clearly plays an important role in this whole dynamic.

Regulation's Impact on Innovation: A Two-Edged Sword

The extent to which the pharmaceutical and medical device industries are regulated has consistently increased over the years.[25] This trend is, at least in part, responsible for the decline in innovative new products (as measured by the number of approved new molecular entities and original premarket approvals). And in the current environment of activist government, the movement toward more regulation and more stringent enforcement seems certain to accelerate.

But there is one aspect of increasing regulation that trumps all others in terms of its potential impact on innovation—comparative effectiveness research.

Why is this likely to have a tremendous impact on innovation? There are two reasons. First, despite assurances to the contrary, comparative effectiveness is almost certain to be used to evaluate the cost effectiveness of alternative treatments. Even if comparative cost data is not collected in the course of research, the outcomes that are measured can be associated with costs after the fact, and given the near-desperate desire of CMS to control the cost of healthcare, it's difficult to envision this move being a long time in coming. That would have a profound impact on the relative risk of innovative and derivative products, and hence on the extent to which innovation occurs.

Second, this represents only the first foray by the US government into comparative effectiveness research. We can count on ongoing, even increasing, effort in this arena, because it does, in fact, pay off. The ability of the UK's National Health Service (NHS) to control costs relies heavily on guidance issued by the National Institute for Health and Clinical Excellence (NICE). This guidance is based on explicit evaluation of the costs and benefits of competing treatments—in other words, on comparative effectiveness research with costs worked into the mix, with the goal of getting the most bang for the pound. And despite the myriad complaints lodged by the British people against NHS, in this respect it has been extremely successful—it currently spends about $2,450 per person per year, compared to about $8,000 per person per year spent on healthcare in the United States.

If the rise of comparative effectiveness research results in the adoption of a set of NICE-style guidelines by CMS, there will be significant negative impacts on innovation. The United States is the largest market in the world for innovative treatments, largely because there is a willingness to pay for them. If CMS starts to weigh cost into its approval process, there will be significantly less willingness to pay.

That translates into increased risk for the developers of innovative new treatments, because it presents a new hurdle to market success—a product no longer has to be merely safe, effective, and appealing to physicians and their patients, now it has to be cost effective as well. Within the NHS, this frequently means that new treatments are rejected or are considered appropriate only under very restricted circumstances. The United Kingdom is a large market for healthcare services, but the United States is much larger; receiving payment at full market price within the United States is extremely important if the developers are to cover the full costs of developing the drug or device, which include the costs of the multiple failures that are typically required before a successful new product comes to market.

By their nature, innovative drugs and devices present more risk of failure than derivative products do, and raising the bar not only increases the chances that any given product will fail, but increases the number of failures each success has to "cover" for the company to maintain profitability. What's more, "successful" products may become less so, on average—strong restrictions on the population for which a product is approved and the circumstances under which it can be used, extremely common in NICE guidelines, greatly reduce the size of the potential market. This makes it even more difficult to recover these costs.

This puts pharmaceutical and medical device companies in a very difficult situation. They need to develop new drugs and devices—that's what they do—but innovative products would become exceptionally risky and uneconomical. Their rational response might be to become high-throughput producers of derivative products, dropping their pursuit of the big innovations, and focusing on products that can make money at a low price point. This implies a bias toward products that can be developed quickly and cheaply, that are likely to have safety profiles similar to currently marketed drugs and devices, and that can find a niche among those who are less-than-perfect candidates for other available options. It creates impetus for innovation in manufacturing processes, rather than products. This is valuable work, but it isn't the kind of innovation that pushes the frontiers of medical treatment.

And it should be noted that this effect applies not only to established companies, but to startups as well. These companies may not rely on profits to fund their research, but they do rely on investors to support their attempts to develop innovative new products. Reducing the expected return on those investments decreases the capital that will be available and the number of small R&D-focused firms that can be supported. One of the most active sources of innovative new products will be significantly impaired.

On the other hand, there is also danger in focusing solely on derivative products. By their nature, they will generally justify only incremental additional reimbursement, and in some cases may not justify additional reimbursement at all. This is especially likely if government decides that there isn't enough "real innovation" going on, or if budgets get very tight.

Companies might respond in two ways. Following the lead of regulators, they will rush to engage in innovation where it is perceived that reimbursement policies are more rewarding. This is likely to be in select product areas where it is difficult for regulators to "just say no" without significant push back from patients' groups.

Alternately, efforts will turn with even more strength than today toward ways to reduce the risk of highly innovative development efforts—toward finding better ways of screening drugs (perhaps through biomarkers), of modeling the durability and performance of devices, and of the interaction of products with the body. This would mean better health outcomes on any budget and would represent an increase in truly valuable innovations. If it succeeds spectacularly, it would usher in a new era of lower-cost innovation in drug and device firms.

The question is, can regulators—through cost-effectiveness research—find the "sweet spot" that encourages increased productivity in the industry? It seems unlikely. The more that cost-containment policy is effective, the more disincentives there are to innovate. Over the long term, as wealthy societies in the United States and Europe age, there will undoubtedly be a backlash against such policies. But in the short and medium term, there are likely to be waves of consolidation and a steep reduction in innovation as the pharmaceutical and medical device industries contract to deal with the government's monopsony pricing power. As in other highly regulated industries, the reduction in competition provides another disincentive to innovate.

The world values innovative new drugs and devices, but it does not value them infinitely, and we are now coming up against the unwillingness of even the most generous public payers to bear their costs. Clinical effectiveness research, and the regulation in other words likely to follow it, is the first step in their systematic plan for saying "no." Depending on how this research is used, it may result in more focused research and development with increased focus on providing real economic and clinical value (though at a significant cost to the total productivity and innovativeness of the industry), or it may create a strong disincentive to product innovation of all kinds. It's a two-edged sword that cuts both ways, but will certainly cut deep.

The only other alternative, which is only hinted at in Europe and some programs in the United States (like Medicare Part D drug coverage for seniors), is to create more market-based incentives that allow consumers to choose between more expensive (but innovative) products and cheaper generics. Wealthier segments of society could also be asked to pay more for healthcare innovations that, over time, become less expensive as they lose patent protection and become more widely adopted. This type of differential pricing strategy has the potential to reconcile the twin goals of cost containment and innovation at a market-clearing price.

Making the Rules Clearer, More Transparent, and Simpler

This is a country of law, of rules. What's at issue in the recent debate over the proper role of the FDA is how far those rules have gone to basically undermine innovation. If you start with the premise that people (and therefore business) can't be trusted, then your goal is to prescribe, in infinite detail, what can and can't be done and then delineate the penalties for noncompliance. Even in Soviet Russia under communist/socialist rule and the real threat of severe penalties, people found ways around rules, with people often paying officials large sums to enable special treatment (in Soviet Russia corruption was widespread). Not that we're suggesting our federal government has become an entirely socialist system—yet. But the move in recent years toward more rules is quite alarming, and it carries with it the real possibility of stifling the very innovation and entrepreneurship that has made this country great.

Too much structure (i.e., rules) stifles freedom and creativity. Too little structure can breed chaos and corruption. We are unfortunately becoming a nation of people watching people to make sure that others don't violate the rules. But often the rules that we do have are not reinforced. The solution is not, as some would suggest, to layer on more rules. The solution, ironically, may be to make the rules clearer, more transparent, and simpler.

Some people in general and some people in business will focus on finding the loopholes to give themselves an advantage. Nothing will be so ironclad as to prevent people from finding ways around onerous rules. So finding the minimally necessary structure or the right level of guidance to balance competing interests and maintain innovation and safety is really what the doctor ordered. Effectively applying this principle to the challenges facing the FDA as it confronts the Prescription Drug User Fee Act (PDUFA) and Medical Device User Fee Act (MDUFA) will be critical to success.

Government has a responsibility to protect its citizens from harm—whether the threat comes from abroad or within. The removal of bureaucratic rules that keep potentially life-saving innovations from reaching their intended audiences is clearly in the spirit of protecting citizens from harm. So, it is in that spirit that we look favorably on recent efforts within the FDA to accelerate the new drug approval process.

Real-Life Example

The FDA's removal of Avastin's indication for breast cancer is a lagging indicator—the FDA was just picking up on what the market had already realized. One could even argue that the revoked approval was redundant, since the market had responded to postapproval studies, as indicated by the fact that use of the drug for treating metastatic breast cancer had plummeted as more data about the drug's limitations became available.

The ability of the market to self-correct supports the case for expanding the accelerated approval process to other therapeutic areas. But herein is the dilemma: Which therapeutic areas get to be a part of the accelerated process?

Who is the government to decide that one drug for say, Alzheimer's disease, has any more right to get to market quicker than a drug for diabetes? And if the market is this responsive to available data, why don't we start utilizing accelerated approval for every drug? If the accelerated approval process is a good enough indicator of safety and efficacy for certain products, then why is it not sufficient for others?

Right now, the accelerated approval process is mainly used for drugs designed to treat cancer or AIDS. It's pretty clear that there is a political upside to making approval requirements less onerous in these two areas—they've both been hot topics in the fifteen years since the Food and Drug Administration Modernization Act (FDAMA) of 1997 passed, codifying the accelerated approval process. But the question becomes whether or not the government should get to decide which areas deserve research the most.

If the accelerated approval process were normative, manufacturers could design clinical studies that rely on data reflecting a real-world evidence approach and modeling, rather than the traditional, large-scale, randomized (placebo-controlled) clinical trials (RCTs) with their associated inclusion/exclusion issues. Instead of waiting years for an actual clinical outcome from RCTs, manufacturers could use a *surrogate endpoint* (like tumor shrinkage, in the case of cancer drugs) to establish an event that can reasonably predict increased survival rate. Drugs would reach the market faster and enable many patients who might otherwise die the opportunity to try a progressive drug.

Additional confirmatory studies would provide longitudinal evidence that the drug either does or does not provide clinical benefits for specific sets of patients, allowing the FDA to react accordingly. Given trends toward personalized medicine, focused clinical studies for narrower patient populations seem more appropriate.

Utilizing accelerated approval could reduce development costs, and pharmaceutical companies could focus their attention on innovating new life-saving therapies, rather than having to funnel all their resources to getting one drug approved. This could revolutionize the industry as we know it.

Patent Life: Shooting Ourselves in the Foot

When you think about the industries where the United States has been preeminent, it's mostly a list of has-beens—steel, autos, and heavy equipment. Those few industries where the United States is still a world leader include pharmaceuticals and medical devices. But this is changing.

As described in Chapter 7, pharmaceutical and medical device manufacturers have seventeen years from the date of patent issuance to make their investment payoff. But having a patent is not the same as having a product. First you need FDA approval.

That's when the real work begins. Experts estimate that it costs over $1 billion and 10 years to bring a new drug to market. Lots of patents never see the commercial light of day. In the earliest stages of discovery; side effects may prove to be problematic and so development stops. Some molecules may fail to perform or have problematic side effects. Drugs that make it to market have to recoup the costs for all the products that failed before them. Finally, CMS must agree to reimburse the product or its potential may be limited.

Given the substantial time and financial commitments required to bring a new drug to market, congressional and public pressure to further reduce the length of patent protection represents a major challenge for the US medical products industry. What most people don't realize is this very pressure puts at risk one of our few remaining industrial jewels.[26] The argument put forth in support of more limited protection is the opportunity to bring generics to market faster and at a significantly lower cost than branded pharmaceuticals.

That generics come at a cheaper price should come as no surprise to anyone. Generic manufacturers don't have to invest in risky R&D, don't bear the brunt of regulatory approval, and don't have the same commercialization costs to bear. But the focus on bringing generics out faster to lower overall healthcare costs misses one critical point.

Pharmaceuticals, while highly visible, represent only about 10% of the cost of healthcare in the United States. And they enable greater productivity on the part of people taking them for the most part! If we're serious about lowering healthcare costs, then we need to look elsewhere.

Finally, increased regulation in this country makes it more difficult to get drugs approved in the first place. So much so that venture capitalists, in evaluating investment opportunities, commonly reject proposals from start-ups who want to launch their new products first in the United States. They regard such plans as reflecting business naiveté.

If the risk to innovation and access to life-saving new compounds isn't significant enough, consider this: 6 million jobs— good jobs—are connected to the pharmaceutical and medical device industry. There was never a time we could afford to put 6 million jobs at risk—and certainly not now.

Endnotes

1. Rita E. Numerof, "Why Accountable Care Organizations Won't Deliver Better Healthcare—and Market Innovation Will," The Heritage Foundation, April 18, 2011.
2. Elliott S. Fisher, Douglas O. Staiger, Julie P. W. Bynum, and Daniel J. Gottlieb, "Creating Accountable Care Organizations," *Health Affairs* 26, no. 1 (2007): 44–57.
3. Fisher et al., "Creating Accountable Care."
4. Kelly Devers and Robert Berenson, "Can Accountable Care Organizations Improve the Value of Health Care by Solving the Cost and Quality Quandaries?" Urban Institute and Robert Wood Johnson Foundation, October 2009, 1–3, http://www.rwjf.org/files/research/acobrieffinal.pdf (accessed March 31, 2011).
5. Fisher et al., "Creating Accountable Care."
6. Devers and Berenson, "Can Accountable Care."
7. Devers and Berenson, "Can Accountable Care."

8. Mark Merlis et al., "Health Policy Brief: Accountable Care Organizations," Robert Wood Johnson Foundation *Health Affairs*, August 13, 2010, 2, http://www.healthaffairs.org/health-policybriefs/brief.php?brief_id=23.

9. Patient Protection and Affordable Care Act of 2009, H.R. 3690, 111th Cong. (2009), Sec. 3022, "Medicare Shared Savings Program."

10. Patient Protection and Affordable Care Act, Sec. 3022, "Medicare Shared Savings Program."

11. Fisher et al., "Creating Accountable Care."

12. Patient Protection and Affordable Care Act, Sec. 3022, "Medicare Shared Savings Program."

13. This influence is not necessarily benign. "The size and power of Medicare are such as to easily distort the healthcare marketplace, the consequences of which will ultimately be harmful to everyone." Harry Cain, "The Medicare Menace," *Harvard Health Policy Review* 2, no. 1 (2001): 20.

14. Tim Brady and Barbie Robinson, "Medicare Hospital Prospective Payment System: How DRG Rates Are Calculated and Updated." U.S. Department of Health and Human Services, Office of Inspector General, Office of Evaluation and Inspections, August 2001, 1–4, http://oig.hhs.gov/oei/reports/oei-09-00-00200.pdf (accessed March 31, 2010).

15. Louise J. Sargent and Renwyck Elder, "Overview of Medicare for Managed Care Professionals," *Journal of Managed Care Pharmacy*, 2, no. 2 (March/April 1996): 165–167, http://www.amcp.org/data/jmcp/Update_165-172.pdf (accessed March 31, 2010).

16. Harry A. Sultz and Kristina M. Young, " Financing Healthcare," in *Health Care USA: Understanding Its Organization and Delivery*, 6th ed. (Sudbury, MA: Jones & Bartlett Learning, 2009), 240–242.

17. Katherine Swartz and Troyen A. Brennan, "Integrated Health Care, Capitated Payment, and Quality: The Role of Regulation," *Annals of Internal Medicine*, 124, no. 4 (1996): 443–444.

18. Rita E. Numerof, "What's Wrong With Healthcare Insurance Exchanges," Galen Institute, May 2012.

19. The Congressional Budget Office (CBO) has estimated enrollment in Medicaid programs will expand from nearly 68.7M in 2013 to 90.1M in 2017. Congressional Budget Office, *The*

Budget and Economic Outlook: Fiscal Years 2012 to 2022 (March 2012). http://www.cbo.gov/sies/default/files/cbofiles/attachments/43059_Medicaid.pdf.

20. There were "only seven state-mandated benefits in 1965; [and in 1997] there are nearly 1,000," according to the National Center for Policy Analysis; see "The Cost of Health Insurance Mandates," Brief Analysis No. 237, August 13, 1997, http://www.ncpa.org/pub/ba237. There were 2,156 mandates reported in 2010, according to the Council for Affordable Health Insurance; see "Health Insurance Mandates in the States 2010," http://www.cahi.org/cahi_contents/newsroom/article.asp?id=1037 (accessed May 5, 2011).

21. Council for Affordable Health Insurance, "Health Insurance Mandates."

22. Catastrophic coverage plans operate more like other types of insurance, e.g., auto, home, life, or personal liability. However, comprehensive coverage plans have become something entirely different: they are used to pay for less-expensive, run-of-the-mill expenses for which consumers can plan, such as regular check-ups, vaccinations, and elective procedures. If auto insurance worked this way, claims would have to be filed, verified, and reimbursed to pay for oil changes or to replace a flat tire. If Americans would rethink the purpose of healthcare insurance, enormous cost could be pulled out of the system. High-deductible health plans and health savings accounts are encouraging more savvy consumer decisions in the purchase of healthcare services.

23. See the St. Louis Regional Chamber and Growth Association website, http://www.stlrcga.org.

24. "Smoking Status and Body Mass Index Relative to Average Individual Health Insurance Premiums," an addendum to the November 2011 eHealth report, "The Cost and Benefits of Individual & Family Health Insurance Plans." The report compared premiums for individuals that fit Centers for Disease Control (CDC) guidelines for obesity based on body mass index scores.

25. "Regulation's Impact on Innovation: A Two-Edged Sword" by Rita E. Numerof, *Medical Progress Today*, May 15, 2009.

26. "Shooting Ourselves in the Foot" by Rita E. Numerof, *Medical Progress Today Blog*, January 21, 2012, http://www.medicalprogresstoday.com/2012/01/shooting-ourselves-in-the-foot.php

Chapter 10

Creating a Roadmap for Change

Revisiting the Challenge of Industry Transition

As we have argued throughout this book, the healthcare industry is clearly an industry in transition. Like other industries that have traveled this route before, healthcare faces unprecedented change. However, unlike others, the assaults are coming simultaneously from all four of the factors that create transition in any industry—significant changes in the regulatory environment, a dynamic and rapidly changing competitive landscape, shifts in technology, and changing market expectations. In the face of this, all industry players must challenge fundamental assumptions about their business models, how they go to market, the types of products and services they offer, the nature of their customer base, and the competencies that will be critical to continued success.

Even under normal circumstances, managing through this set of changes is hard. When all four forces descend at once, successful navigation becomes that much harder. Not surprisingly, there is enormous resistance to the needed changes. On the face of it, the resistance makes sense. Organizations have built infrastructure to support their current business model, and staff have been rewarded and promoted on the basis of it. Investments in the model have generally paid off. To make things harder, the current business model is still throwing off cash. So the challenge comes down to building the new amid uncertainty and general turbulence, while generating revenue from the old.

Despite the warning signs that the road ahead is "out" and a detour needs to be taken quickly, the momentum of the current way of doing business is so intense that it's going to be hard for many to avoid going over the cliff.

We have needed healthcare reform in this country. For the reasons we've outlined, the industry sectors didn't take needed action to fix serious problems when they could. In the face of the Patient Protection and Affordable Care Act (PPACA) they have been forced to. And the dust hasn't yet begun to settle. As one industry executive recently put it,

> PPACA was a bullet to my head. ... Our entire indus-
> try had opportunity after opportunity to fix the prob-
> lems facing us—lack of customer responsiveness,
> lack of transparency, lack of efficiency, lack of ser-
> vice integration, lack of meaningful choice—and we
> essentially chose to do nothing about it. Our future
> survival depends on our ability to reinvent ourselves
> ... and some of us are unlikely to make it.

A sobering thought, and one we hear expressed often from industry executives—behind closed doors. PPACA, regardless of the view one has of the legislation, has created enormous disruption, and with it comes enormous opportunity as well as risk.

Unfortunately, we have proven ourselves capable of only suboptimal solutions to date. Without real clarity on the goal and an overarching, integrated strategy for how to realize it, with lots of choice in the process, we won't get the result we need. PPACA is both too prescriptive and not sufficiently strategic. It's a Rube Goldberg contraption that essentially doesn't work.

The debate around the constitutionality of the individual mandate, really concerns fundamental issues in regard to the legitimate role of government in our society. At one level, PPACA compels people to enter into a contract that's not necessarily in their own self-interest in order to subsidize others. It is a classic case of wealth transfer—confiscating individuals' earned assets or prerogatives by the government to redistribute them to those deemed more worthy. As David Brooks (columnist for the *New York Times*) pointed out on *Meet the Press* on April 1, 2012, the law represents another step toward centralization of power in the federal government.

He suggested that as an alternative and a general philosophy, the government could have defined the overall goal and then left it to the states and individuals to figure out how to get there. This is exactly the position we've been arguing for the last several years. Unfortunately, the options presented to date have been polarized—a universal, single-payer system with prescribed Cadillac mandates provided by the private sector under the thumb of the central government, overseen by a 15-person Independent Payment Advisory Board (IPAB) operating outside any congressional oversight.

Most people in this country would agree that providing some form of basic coverage for all in need is the mark of a good society. In other countries, including Australia, government provides a base level of coverage for all of its citizens with private insurance coverage layering options on top. What's included in that base has been hotly debated in the United States. Even though the country is a meritocracy, there are progressive threads that find the idea of a multi-tiered system abhorrent. Some have the view that "everyone among us deserves the same," and anything else is unfair. With unlimited dollars, this approach might be desirable. However, as we've pointed out, we don't have unlimited dollars, and with the "silver tsunami" forming, we don't have much time to fix the problem.

Establishing the central goal might have worked if the Centers for Medicare and Medicaid Services (CMS) had said, "We're not going to pay for never events; we're going to tie payment to outcomes." They had the authority to do it, and for the reasons discussed here, didn't. PPACA gave them the political cover to do it, but ironically, any real teeth have been taken out.

Part of the dilution has come from pressure from the delivery sector and a lack of real spine on the part of the political establishment. The political reality of healthcare delivery and how money flows deserves comment here. In many communities, hospitals are the largest employers and large campaign contributors. People are dependent on these employers for jobs, and as importantly, for their well-being as healthcare providers when they're sick. So, the idea of applying real pressure for fundamental change is a tricky proposition. The irony is that in many of these organizations, people at the top are paid richly and their organizations receive substantial subsidies from the government, while at the same time they decry the lack of reimbursement and their inability to redesign their business models.

Understanding the money flow helps to engage in a productive dialogue, allowing consumers to be better at consuming and business leaders to be wiser business professionals. Clearly, delivery organizations alone can't mount the changes that are needed. The basis for payment needs to change, and they own one key part of the puzzle. Real solutions will require collaboration among industry players in local markets. We're all part of the problem, and we all need to be part of the solution. Unfortunately, the dominant moves in the industry have been consistent with the current business model.

Safety in Size? The Rush to Affiliation

As has been true in years past, industry consolidation and attempts to leverage size and scale have been used to stave off competitive threat. In the 1990s, hospitals embarked on massive affiliations and buying sprees. Hospitals scooped up primary care practices, often as a defensive maneuver to protect the referral base for lucrative specialty services. A great many of those ventures didn't pan out as expected. Some hospital systems overpaid for the assets they bought. Still others couldn't get the productivity gains they'd envisioned, learning the hard way that employed physicians aren't the same as private practice doctors, and managing small businesses requires a nimbleness and focus that most large, siloed bureaucratic institutions couldn't master. Not unlike other mergers or acquisitions across industries, the failure rate was quite high, frequently due to cultural incompatibility.

We're likely to see a repeat of the 1990s in the next five years unless better discipline is applied to the hard work of merger and acquisition integration. We're already seeing physicians exiting private practices in droves to become hospital employees. But remember, getting the deal inked is typically the easy part.

What most healthcare systems, payers, and manufacturers don't realize, however, is that the real threat comes from not-in-kind competition, as we've described earlier. So scale and competitive consolidation that rely on the current business model will only offer temporary respite from the real disruptive innovation lurking around the corner. As we described in Chapter 1, Walgreens and Walmart have begun to take steps to sell insurance and offer retail healthcare services through in-store clinics. Even supermarkets are dipping their toes into the healthcare business, capitalizing on convenience, price, choice, and ease of use.

These major retailers represent a threat to the way things have been. They've successfully shaken up prescription drug pricing by offering generics at very low prices. They understand negotiation in a way that insurers and hospitals don't. They understand outcomes and move quickly in response to market needs. The problems of unpredictable costs and inefficient management of chronic illness could be the very problems firms like these are ready to tackle. What happens when retail chains jump into the mix and start offering health insurance or when the Progressive model for car insurance changes the dynamics for this insurance market?

It is likely that in the short run hospitals will join forces and use their size as a competitive deterrent. Smaller stand-alone hospital groups find affiliations with larger, better financed organizations attractive in the face of increasing regulation and changes in how hospitals will be paid. Whereas size has historically been used to extract higher payments from insurers, it's unlikely to be the case today. Hospitals must become more efficient in the face of reduced reimbursement from Medicare and other insurers, more transparent and more consumer centered. They must also demonstrate the economic and clinical value of what they offer compared to alternatives and answer the question, why should anyone come to their institution?

Insurers are dipping their toes in the water and looking to acquire healthcare delivery organizations; health and disease management companies; research, IT, and health outcomes organizations; and pharmacy benefit manager (PBMs). As an example on the delivery side, UnitedHealth Group (UHG) went on a buying spree in 2011, purchasing Monarch Healthcare, Memorial, and AppleCare, all California-based delivery groups, and Southwest Medical Associates, based in Nevada. In 2005, UHG bought PacifiCare Health System, a California insurance plan provider. On the opposite coast, Highmark, a large Pennsylvania-based insurer, has teamed up with West Penn Allegheny Health System (this deal was to be reviewed by the Pennsylvania Insurance Department in April 2012). The move is aimed at competing more successfully with the University of Pittsburgh Medical Center (UPMC), the large, well-known academic medical center in Pittsburgh. A driving force behind this is the exercise of more control over practice patterns and ultimately cost.

One of the real concerns this raises in the short run is the massive consolidation of power in a few very large players, limiting choice and accountability. Similarly, it raises the question: are they getting too big to fail, or worse yet, too big to care? Private equity firms have also entered the game. Oak Hill Capital Partners established a partnership with St. Louis-based Ascension Health to buy Catholic hospitals around the country. Others who are looking to get into the market are sitting on the sidelines, evaluating how these new arrangements perform financially.

Consolidation and the Challenge for Manufacturers

These moves will have significant and likely negative implications for manufacturers selling into the delivery sector. With size comes greater purchasing power and the ability to extract price concessions from manufacturers wanting to sell their goods and services into these organizations. Increasingly, we expect to see downward price pressure, accelerated consolidation, and fewer suppliers serving specific markets—a trend that began in earnest in 2010. Unless manufacturers can demonstrate the economic and clinical value of their product in relation to alternative products and therapeutic options, the commoditization trend will accelerate.

Some industry observers, including Moody's, see these shifts as good for the industry. Moody's suggests that insurers need to start thinking about themselves as a one-stop shop. These kinds of moves, they argue, can enable greater competitiveness as they look to create networks of hospitals and doctors responsible for delivering and coordinating care in large communities. It sounds a lot like the government's plan for accountable care organizations (ACOs), which we discussed in Chapter 9. Unlike the government's plan, this one is being initiated by the market and is insurer driven rather than provider driven. Like the government plan, it erroneously assumes that bigger will be more efficient and effective. But none of the players has created a new business model, so it's unlikely that consolidation will result in a better solution. In fact, Moody's correctly notes that such consolidation will present fewer choices to patients in any given market, but they go on to suggest that size might result in a stronger system financially. That strength, in turn, *could* deliver better quality at lower cost. Given past history, it's unlikely.

The problem with this approach is consolidation of power in some of the very institutions that have brought us to the brink. Insurers have not been patient centered, let alone consumer centered. Large delivery organizations have not been efficient, integrated, or consumer centered. They have been guilty of upcoding, being opaque in their charges, and adding unnecessary services. Moreover, their service processes haven't generally centered on the patient/consumer. Ownership by insurers, who are committed to reducing unneeded services, has the potential to address cost, but only if the fundamental business model of both sectors changes. So far we haven't seen demonstrations of such leadership.

Those large healthcare delivery organizations that have successfully mastered the challenge of managing variation in cost and quality—like Kaiser, Cleveland Clinic, and Geisinger, among others—have invested millions of dollars annually in building the IT infrastructure, but more importantly have committed to compliance to agreed upon care paths across a broader continuum of care approach. Such change is not for the faint of heart or conflict avoidant among us.

In some respects, creating an ACO to achieve clinical and financial integration is naïve. No one told Microsoft to acquire companies and combine under one umbrella, or J&J to become a diverse holding company with products ranging from baby shampoo and Band-Aids to complex medical devices, diagnostics, and pharmaceutical and biotech agents.

Nor was Boeing directed to make all of the components of its new aircraft itself. Indeed, in every market, successful companies have engaged selectively and strategically with partners that shared a common vision. Their strategic alliances, strategic partnerships, or joint ventures succeeded or failed on the clarity of the vision, the rigor of execution, the commitment to a common purpose and shared culture. None was successful because it was legally *mandated*.

Additional Challenges for Manufacturers

Manufacturers not only have to figure out how to address their changing customer base, they are also under significant pressure in light of a hostile business environment. The pharmaceutical industry, in particular, has been the common target of a convenient alliance of media, government, and academia, each with its own agenda. It has been accused of, among other things, influencing physicians for purely commercial reasons—in some cases bringing products with dubious value to market, creating demand for drugs to treat conditions of questionable medical need, withholding clinical data that would position products in a less than optimal light, and using continuing medical education (CME) for commercial promotion as opposed to balanced objective education. The general lack of real evidence behind many of the accusations, the tendency to generalize from specific details to the whole, and a generally nonscientific approach to the underlying controversy has had the continuing feel of a political witch hunt gathering momentum.

As an example, a vocal academic minority believes that industry can never add value to CME and should be out of the business altogether, except for its "obligation" to pay for CME (and related grants) through an undifferentiated common pool of funds that others would administer. But let's face it—every sector, every professional, every individual has a bias.

Critics make the assumption that any commercial interest in the mix taints objectivity and negates any legitimate value. The further assumption that commercial interests are the only source of bias is simplistic. Many of the actors in the healthcare debate have underlying agendas related to control of power and resources, and some of the extreme positions taken reflect a broader antibusiness orientation in other words increasingly common in the current political dialogue.

Creating Collaborations to Develop Lifetime Value

Collaborations are where the opportunity lies. It will be up to manufacturers to design—on the basis of a rich understanding of the interactions between disease states, lifestyle variables, and the characteristics of their products—interventions that provide maximum clinical and economic value over the lifetime of a patient. These interventions are likely to incorporate service wraps and other inherently differentiating features that boost the effectiveness of the core products and enhance their value.

Demonstrating this enhanced value will require studies that take into account the expected downstream impacts of an intervention and allow quantification of these benefits in a comprehensive fashion. Their focus will be longer term and the outcome measures more complex than are common today. There are implications for the scope of interventions as well; for example, a monitored, structured lifestyle change program might be necessary to maximize the lifetime value of an intervention, which would effectively render it a part of a manufacturer's offering.

It will also fall to manufacturers to shape the understanding of insurers, patients, and physicians regarding this approach. Ultimately, the case that manufacturers would like to make is that the entirety of benefits accruing to an intervention should be reflected in the valuation of that intervention and weighed against its costs. This would justify premium pricing and help to avoid what might otherwise become the default position for payers, and increasingly a position being taken by large provider organizations—a preference for the least expensive intervention that alleviates the currently salient problem, an approach that could well be "penny wise and pound foolish."

The good news is that payers, physicians, and patients are primed to accept a lifetime value orientation—they've been saying for more than twenty years that prevention is less costly than treatment, so they can hardly object to the idea that downstream impacts are important. The bad news is that this imposes a heavy burden of proof on manufacturers. Outcome studies are risky endeavors with large uncertainties regarding the size of the economic and quality-of-life impacts that can be expected downstream. The burden may be too heavy to bear unless patients, physicians, and especially payers make commitments to collaboration.

Manufacturers, however, have something of value that can be traded for these accommodations—the ability to focus their efforts on the development of supremely cost-effective treatments. That key point of leverage needs to be used to convince other parties that requiring absolute proof of the lifetime benefits of an intervention before approving payment is not in anyone's best interests—it will stifle the development of these ultimately more cost-effective and innovative approaches. Instead, they should support efforts based on agreed upon methods for estimating those downstream impacts, with the true value to be determined over time as actual patient records become available, essentially elevating the importance of post-market studies.

Many insurers already have systems for tracking patient outcomes in place (Kaiser Permanente is perhaps the most advanced on this front) and are well positioned to aid in these efforts. With its focus on long-term outcomes, CMS would be another logical initial partner, as would large nationalized or seminationalized healthcare systems in the United Kingdom, Australia, and Canada.

For manufacturers, the approach will be to devise a set of quantitative models that represent best estimates regarding the downstream impacts. These models, which would capture the causal pathways linking disease states, lifestyle, and treatment variables, would serve as the basis for estimating the full economic and clinical impacts of an intervention and could also help to guide the search for evidence by specifying the outcome measures of primary interest. These models would be vetted with payers, which would agree to value a limited number of interventions prospectively on the basis of the predicted downstream benefits.

Why Now?

The lifetime value approach is simple, almost obvious, but it hasn't made major inroads yet—the pressure required to move the various elements of the healthcare industry toward it simply didn't exist. Today, however, the pressure is on, and it continues to mount. The time is right for manufacturers and insurers to make the leap.

The approach is entirely ethical—it is a pure attempt to deliver better health outcomes with maximum efficiency. The end result will be sustainable differentiation of interventions, a more efficient, cost-effective healthcare system, and improved outcomes when viewed from the perspective of the continuum of care. It's a powerful case to make, and one that needs to be made today.

Reprising the Consumer

From our perspective, much of the resistance to real healthcare reform in this country stems from the reluctance of market players to envision another world—another world in which the consumer is at the center, not the insurer, not the physician, and not the hospital. As the business model shifts to a consumer orientation, those players who have long dominated the healthcare marketplace will be challenged by market leaders that are more nimble and retail savvy. We anticipate that over the next several years, despite PPACA's attempt to define comprehensive, universal health benefits as an entitlement, the move to a defined contribution—by both employers and government subsidies—will encourage more personal choice. The market will move from a wholesale model to a retail model, the former focused on the employer/corporation, the latter on the individual consumer.

With this shift will come a change in core competencies. As we discussed in prior chapters, real customer service will become king, characterized by availability, 24/7 access support, broad choice, and customized services to meet the unique needs of specific customer segments.

Power of Choice

One general strategy for producing net positive value to physicians, patients, or payers is to provide them with choices. Presumably, people will pick the option with greater value—at least that's what economists tell us—so if hospitals add an option no one is worse off, and some people are better off. As a practical matter, of course, there may be additional costs associated with providing extra options, and this may even make both options more expensive, but the general principle is still sound. Offering choices generally increases the value you provide.

But what kinds of choices can hospitals offer? A number of hospitals and hospital systems (such as Alegent in Omaha, Nebraska, and Memorial Health System in South Bend, Indiana) have decided that one choice they can offer is *where* patients engage with medical services. They have opened walk-in clinics in places like convenience stores, grocery stores, and gas stations. Easily accessible and offering extended hours, these clinics give patients a way to have simple diagnostic tests performed on their own schedule. They give worried parents of ailing children an alternative to phone tag with on-call doctors and "can you come in at 2:00 tomorrow afternoon?", and give those without a primary care physician an alternative to appearing at the emergency room door for a sore throat, pinkeye, or common earache. Those who use them love them, and many happily forgo coverage under their insurance for the convenience the clinics provide (though many such clinics do accept insurance). They aren't for everyone, but then, no one has to use them. That's the beauty of choice.

But choice doesn't have to be limited to where people seek care. *How* hospitals provide care and *what kind* of care they provide can also be points of differentiation. Would patients be willing to pay more out of pocket for a single room? Some of them would, a point that hasn't been lost on US hospitals for many years. A hospital in Canada, by way of example, takes the idea a step further. Toronto East General Hospital in Ontario, Canada offers patients the option to upgrade from standard rooms to semiprivate, private, or private deluxe rooms, and posts the nightly charge on its website. It's a relatively easy thing for Toronto East to do because virtually every patient they see has the same coverage, but the calculations that would be required to offer similar options in the United States are hardly prohibitive. And room upgrades are just the beginning—the opportunities for premium services are virtually unlimited. Premium food, bedside Internet access, frequent visits by friendly faces—all of them might prove popular with patients, and all have the potential to be very profitable.

For those concerned about an increase in enforced cost effectiveness, whether from consumer-directed healthcare, reinvigorated managed care plans, or a desperate CMS, creating choices now will help in two ways. First, it will provide a source of revenue independent of reimbursement—the less they pay for, the more opportunities there are to offer premium services. In the longer term, by getting into the game of providing "by choice" premium services directly to patients, hospitals will be situated to take advantage of premium private insurance plans (like those that have sprung up around other nationalized healthcare systems) should universal healthcare become a reality.

Increase Perceived Quality

Another way to increase value, and physicians may be especially appropriate targets of this kind of differentiation, is to increase perceived quality of care. Hospitals might, for example, select a set of highly salient outcome measures, work to become world class on those measures, and market their outcomes. Metrics might include recovery times, complication rates, and rates of hospital-contracted infections. Volume within a given diagnosis can be a differentiator in the minds of physicians, because experience is associated with competence, and a similar argument can be made for the creation and marketing of *super teams* within a specialty.

Efforts to increase the perceived quality of offerings can also be directed at patients. There may, for example, be opportunities to restructure, or simply re-explain, care delivery so that it makes sense to them. The ability to tell a coherent story about *why* a service works the way it does is a major differentiator of successful firms in most service-providing industries. When auto rental companies advertise that "they'll pick you up," so renters don't have to figure out a way to get to the rental office, or financial services firms explain that they provide personal financial planning services to ensure that their clients' investments are structured to meet their needs, they create a reason for customers to voluntarily choose them despite a price premium. If hospitals can tell a similar story about cardiovascular care—a "we'll do these tests and you'll talk to these people because" story—they can also increase the perception of quality and command a premium. This is especially true for the first hospital to create such a coherent story.

As is the case with offering increased choice, increasing the perceived quality of services positions healthcare systems to thrive in a world in other words increasingly concerned with cost effectiveness. At the very least it creates a compelling argument that their treatment is worth a premium.

Competing on value may be more difficult than competing on cost, but it offers opportunities for sustainable differentiation, improved relations with others in the healthcare community (including patients), new revenue streams, and better margins. And it is being done today, in many places, in many ways. Ultimately, the value provided by hospitals (and other healthcare providers) goes beyond standardized care at the lowest cost. It means finding ways to provide more. More choice, better service, and increased convenience are the first places to look.

Creating and Sustaining a New Business Model

It's hard for any organization to conceptualize a new business model, especially when meeting the current plan is getting increasingly difficult in a dynamic market. This is the work of executive leaders. Only they can envision a different future and make the difficult decisions required to reconfigure their organization to achieve its new vision. This cannot be accomplished over the course of a few weeks of focused planning meetings. It's ongoing executive leadership work that must remain a top priority, even while these same leaders are also running their current business in other words still expected to grow and remain profitable.

Once envisioned, a new business model must be embedded into the organization. This is an equally difficult aspect of creating and sustaining a new business model. A company is reliant on its managers for such change, and they are steeped in the old business model. Managers are usually promoted on the basis of strong technical skills and the ability to execute efficiently within the existing structure and business model. As a result, many managers are likely to lack the managerial skills that allow them to drive change through the organization, and are often exceptionally resistant to changing the system that has worked so well for them.

True managers need an understanding of their role in the organization that goes beyond technical expertise to encompass things like strategy-directed corporate stewardship. They need to understand where the organization is going and what their role will be in getting there. Without redefining the role of management, and providing the training and tools to support it, most current managers will never reach that point. As healthcare industry leaders act to change their business models, they need to give more attention to the management infrastructure necessary to implement and sustain it.

Harnessing Consumer Choice and Competition to Ensure Accountability: Final Thoughts for Policymakers

As we've discussed throughout this book, initiatives that rely on complex organizational experiments to build accountability are not only likely to fail, they are also likely to increase costs. Instead, policymakers should establish market conditions where innovative accountable organizations can flourish in a competitive environment, driven by consumer choice. It's easy to imagine how, in such an environment, organizations that are responsive and accountable to patients could flourish. They can focus on prevention, cost efficiency, and improved outcomes and rely on market incentives to enhance accountability across the care continuum.

Imagining a New Market. While PPACA provides health insurance for Americans who previously lacked coverage, it does so at enormous cost and will exacerbate the trend of provider consolidation, thereby reducing competition, and lead to greater inefficiency, less innovation, and ultimately less access to healthcare for consumers. Achieving better health outcomes at lower cost can be accomplished by eliminating perverse financial incentives and unnecessary bureaucracy. Replacing PPACA with legislation that would provide robust free-market choice and real competition would transform the delivery of healthcare. Market pressures would stimulate organizations to deliver better health outcomes at lower cost.

In a free market for health plans and providers, competing organizations will have powerful incentives to pay for healthcare delivery that reflects predictive care paths and evidence-based medicine. Providers *and* healthcare delivery organizations would be required to demonstrate that their services deliver economic and clinical value. To create accountability, healthcare delivery organizations would address variation in treatment practices and inefficiencies in care delivery. Establishing predictive care paths and effectively using evidence-based medicine would help providers and organizations achieve better quality and cost-effective health outcomes.

Properly used, clinical effectiveness research would be integral to assessing the value of various procedures, care paths, and strategies. Providers and the organizations with which they are affiliated would need to provide evidence to support the value of the care they administer before they can expect to be reimbursed for their services.

Using predictive care paths and evidence-based medicine would lead to effective treatment approaches that are good for all stakeholders—patients, physicians, and organizations. These policies would help improve outcomes, establish efficiencies, reduce variations in treatment patterns, and create baselines for determining effectiveness. Instead of the standard top-down administrative payment arrangements, modeled on Medicare, primary care physicians would replace resource-based relative-value units (RBRVUs) with a time-based and outcome-based approach that reflects real prices, market value, and transparency.

Securing better healthcare at lower cost will involve changing the wrong-headed financial incentives and bureaucracy characterizing the present third-party payment system that dominates both the public and private sectors.

Within every organization in a competitive and transparent environment, financial incentives that reward quality outcomes will be critical to improving quality of care and gaining market share. Primary care physicians would be able to take a leadership role in ensuring accountability for care; primary care physicians would be able to spend the appropriate amount of time required to accurately diagnose patients and focus on achieving better outcomes. The incentive to subject patients to tests or other procedures that may not be helpful is removed. This approach will also remove the incentives that drive specialists to conduct unnecessary medical procedures by creating counterincentives to work across the care continuum to achieve improved healthcare.

The rapid evolution of the current system toward these types of organizational arrangements will not take place until federal and state policymakers eliminate the existing barriers to private health insurance competition and create a truly competitive marketplace by giving patient-consumers direct control of both healthcare dollars and decisions. In a transparent, information-driven environment, doctors would need to compete for patients, and those who follow predictive care paths and use evidence-based medicine to provide quality care in a cost-effective and transparent manner should succeed.

A truly competitive space provides smaller businesses with the same opportunity to flourish and achieve market share as large organizations. Each must be able to demonstrate accountability for its role in delivering integrated and coordinated care.

In order to achieve such a level playing field, policymakers must break down the barriers to private insurance competition by increasing transparency, accessibility to market information and data, and consumer education while preventing patient discrimination and inappropriate denial of coverage. Doing so empowers the *real* consumers—patients—to make informed decisions about the healthcare for which they are ultimately paying. Informing patients and letting them shop around for the coverage that best meets their needs will ultimately lead to increased demand for better outcomes, an emphasis on prevention and health maintenance, and lower premiums.

End Game

At its most basic level, adapting to a changing landscape means a shift in thinking from simply controlling costs to actively seeking growth *by doing business differently.* Competing in this market is a new game. It will take a redefinition of customers, products, and value propositions. And it will require the development of competencies and management infrastructure to create and sustain an environment where entrepreneurial activity can flourish.

1: The end game is better health outcomes at lower cost. It will only happen if consumers are empowered to make better choices and incented to do so. 2: Twenty-first-century solutions to healthcare will reflect collaboration and innovation in the business models of each sector. 3: Most importantly it will require a level of integration and coordination among disparate previously siloed players in the industry—manufacturers, payers, and healthcare delivery providers working in concert with savvy consumers and 4: This is reflected in the intersection of the Venn diagram in Figure 10.1.

The end game can't be prescribed by governments—either at the state or federal level. Government can help enable this

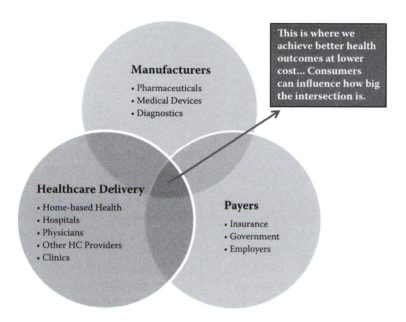

Figure 10.1 The twenty-first-century model for healthcare. (Courtesy of Numerof & Associates, Inc.)

process but it can't mandate it. It can establish the goals and create powerful incentives for change. Success requires every one of us to drive real change. If we do, we'll all be winners. The model of healthcare tomorrow is highly connected, highly integrated, information rich and technology enabled. And it is the consumer who ultimately will determine the outcome.

Creating a twenty-first-century model for healthcare means creating value in healthcare—achieving better health outcomes at lower cost—and it requires transparency and greater consistency in reporting outcomes. But transparency and outcomes have to be tied to financial incentives for better performance. We are all in this together. Improving quality of care, reducing error, fostering prevention, and ensuring efficient treatment will require the engagement of all stakeholders in a new partnership for better health.

The future is possible.

Index

About the Authors

Rita E. Numerof, Ph.D., President of Numerof & Associates, Inc., is an internationally recognized consultant and author with more than twenty-five years of experience in the field of strategy development and execution, business model design, and market analysis.

Her clients have included Fortune 500 companies such as Johnson & Johnson, Eli Lilly, Pfizer, Westinghouse, AstraZeneca, Merck, Abbott Laboratories, major healthcare institutions, payers, and government agencies. The focus of her consulting addresses the challenges of maintaining competitive advantage in highly dynamic and regulated markets.

Dr. Numerof has been a consistent advocate for the importance of strategic differentiation, organizational alignment of structure, competencies and metrics to ensure effective implementation, and anticipating, rather than reacting to industry trends. She's been a pioneer in the area of economic and clinical value, anticipating the impact of changing global

245

payer attitudes on the fundamental business model of the healthcare industry. Her work across the entire healthcare spectrum gives her a unique perspective on the challenges and needs of manufacturers, physicians, payers, and healthcare delivery institutions.

Under her leadership, NAI has developed proprietary approaches that provide precise insight and practical solutions to some of the industry's most complex business challenges. Taking a systemic approach, Dr. Numerof has addressed such diverse issues as comparative effectiveness research, accountable care, bundled pricing, consumer engagement, operationalizing compliance and transparency, portfolio management and the identification of growth platforms that provide sustainable differentiation through economic and clinical value, and effective commercialization based on value propositions that matter to key constituencies.

Dr. Numerof is widely published in business journals and has authored five books. She serves as an advisor to members of Congress on healthcare reform and comparative effectiveness research. She was a senior advisor with the Center for Health Transformation, a regular contributor to the Manhattan Institute, and wrote the Heritage Foundation's policy paper, "Why Accountable Care Organizations Won't Deliver Better Healthcare—and Market Innovation Will." She led a tripartisan, cross-industry work group on payment reform and developed recommendations for new payment models that incent better health outcomes at lower cost. In addition, Dr. Numerof provides guidance to policy organizations and agencies on the relationship between innovation and regulation, working to support innovation and ensure responsive regulatory oversight.

Dr. Numerof graduated magna cum laude from the Honors College, Syracuse University and received her MSS and PhD from Bryn Mawr College.

Michael N. Abrams, M.A., Cofounder and Managing Partner of Numerof & Associates, Inc., has served as an internal and external consultant to Fortune 50 corporations, major pharmaceutical and medical device companies, healthcare delivery institutions, the financial services industry, and government agencies for over twenty-five years. He has worked extensively in the areas of strategic planning and implementation, product strategy and portfolio development, market analysis, consumer engagement, and operational improvement.

Abrams is well known for his expertise in the design and implementation of strategies for building competitive differentiation, defining sustainable value, identifying market influence mechanisms, and translating white space analysis into the creation of innovative solutions to meet unmet needs. His ability to identify market opportunities and to effectively improve organizational performance has been an invaluable resource to client companies on a global basis across industries.

Abrams has structured and managed innovative programs to evaluate care delivery and payment models, thereby defining the internal change processes necessary to translate business opportunities into effective market position, operations, product portfolio management, and new product design consistent with changing regulatory requirements. He has provided solutions to healthcare delivery systems to improve the management of care transitions, thereby reducing unnecessary hospitalizations, and reduced length of stay by identifying and managing factors causing extended stays, changing admissions and patient care management processes, and managing across the continuum of care while maintaining or improving clinical outcomes and reducing costs.

He is experienced in the design and execution of econometric modeling and analysis and decision support systems for a variety of science-driven industries and applications. He has designed technology solutions to meet a wide range of needs, including strategic account planning and management, thought leader interface, and key opinion leader management. His ability to manage the process of technology integration to support business objectives across multiple business environments ensures return on investment (ROI).

Abrams has written extensively on economic and clinical value creation and the need for integrated, systemic solutions to the challenges facing the global healthcare industry. His articles have appeared in more than a dozen leading business journals, and he coauthored the book *Solving the Healthcare Crisis*. As an adjunct faculty member of Washington University in St. Louis and LaSalle College School of Business Administration in Philadelphia, Abrams has taught MBA courses in strategic management, product planning and evaluation, quantitative decision making, and market analysis.

Michael Abrams completed his doctoral work in Business Policy at St. Louis University. He received his MA from George Washington University in Washington, DC.

About NAI

Numerof & Associates, Inc. is a strategic management consulting firm focused on organizations in dynamic, rapidly changing industries like healthcare. For over 25 years, we've helped major pharmaceutical, medical device and diagnostics companies, academic and community health systems, and payers address the strategic and operational challenges to profitable growth and global market leadership. Our work across the entire healthcare spectrum provides us with unique capabilities to develop systemic, customized client solutions. We help clients with three broad types of issues:

- strategy development and execution, closing the gap between where they are and where they need to be;
- operational excellence, addressing core processes in critical functional and operational areas; and
- organizational infrastructure, building enterprise-wide processes that create and sustain excellence.

We believe that periods of economic turbulence present the opportunity to gain competitive advantage and increase market share... with the right strategy, well executed. We bring a dual focus on strategy and execution, helping our clients to ensure that they are working toward a clearly defined set of strategic goals, and that they have the alignment, infrastructure, and capabilities in place to achieve them.

We've been leaders in defining the role of economic and clinical value in developing sustainable differentiation, and in helping clients redesign their business models to capitalize on such changes. Operationalizing such profound strategic shifts requires challenging assumptions and developing new approaches to key parts of the business—from pricing and bundled payment, to clinical integration and new delivery models, to marketing and portfolio management, to commercialization and M&A processes. If you are looking for consultative support in preparing your organization for a rapidly changing business environment, we would like to talk to you.